A Clinician's Guide to

HEALING THE WOUNDS OF RACIAL TRAUMA

A 12-SESSION
CBT-BASED
PROTOCOL

MONNICA T. WILLIAMS, PhD, ABPP

A CLINICIAN'S GUIDE TO HEALING THE WOUNDS OF RACIAL TRAUMA

Published by
PESI Publishing, Inc.
3839 White Ave
Eau Claire, WI 54703

Cover and interior design by Emily Dyer
Cover design adapted from original illustration by Rehman Abdulrehman, PhD
Editing by Jenessa Jackson, PhD

ISBN 9781683737841 (print)
ISBN 9781683737858 (ePUB)
ISBN 9781683737865 (ePDF)

Printed in the United States of America.

Table of Contents

List of Exercises

List of Forms

Introduction

Racial trauma is a common but underrecognized syndrome affecting millions of people of color in the Western world. Racial trauma refers to the severe mental and emotional injury caused by a multitude of experiences of racism compounded over a person's lifetime. When experienced, racial trauma can mimic the severity and symptomatology of posttraumatic stress disorder (PTSD), resulting in flashbacks, recurrent nightmares, avoidance behaviors, embarrassment, isolation, dysphoria, and alterations in arousal and reactivity. Up to 30 percent of Black, Indigenous, and other people of color (BIPOC) may be suffering from varying degrees of racial trauma, and many seek out the help of mental health professionals for treatment (Williams, Osman, et al., 2022). Unfortunately, when these clients present in therapy, clinicians are often at a loss as to how to appropriately treat them. For one, many clinicians lack awareness or knowledge of the harmful impact of racial discrimination on people of color, so they fail to recognize the signs and symptoms. Other clinicians are anxious or uncomfortable holding space for topics of racism within session or do so in a way that is potentially harmful to clients.

The reality is that most White people misunderstand the nature of racism, as they were taught as children that the way to be non-racist is to *not* talk about racism, even when racial issues are pressing. Further, too many clinician training programs fail to provide training in how to discuss racial issues. This has left many therapists without the skills needed to engage in critical conversations with traumatized clients of color. When provocative racial material arises, it is not uncommon for therapists to respond with agitation, anxiety, or confusion. Even therapists who are comfortable talking to clients about racial issues usually haven't learned how to treat racial trauma because this topic is rarely taught in graduate training programs. For example, one study found that although 71 percent of counselors have encountered clients with racial trauma in their practice, less than one in five have received training on how to treat it (Hemmings & Evans, 2018).

Racism is indeed stressful and can be traumatizing. If you are a therapist working with people of color, you must be equipped to treat these clients in an effective and culturally informed manner. This is especially the case given that clinicians can expect to see an ongoing increase in the number of clients of color seeking care. For example, the US Census Bureau (2015) projects that by 2044, non-Hispanic White people will no longer be the majority population. Moreover, by 2031, Canada's current racialized population will make up about a third of the nation's population (Statistics Canada, 2011). As a result, clinicians have an ethical responsibility to be practicing with consideration for the increasingly racially, ethnically, and culturally diverse people who need care. This includes people who identify as Black, Latin American, Asian, Native American, Indigenous, Middle Eastern, non-White international, or multiethnic.

That is where this treatment manual comes in. In this book, I describe the essential ingredients needed to successfully treat racial stress and trauma from a cognitive behavioral therapy (CBT) perspective. This approach is rooted in research I have been conducting internationally for two decades and have tested in my clinical Laboratory for Mental Health Disparities at the University of Ottawa, where I serve as a professor and Canada Research Chair. Called the *healing racial trauma protocol*, it consists of step-by-step guided sessions, each 60 minutes in length, designed to take place over a 12-week period. In addition to being grounded in CBT, the protocol has roots in functional analytic psychotherapy (FAP) and acceptance and commitment therapy (ACT).

The protocol can be broken into three phases: (1) *stabilization and support*, which focuses on providing support to clients in distress; (2) *healing*, which emphasizes cognitive restructuring and exposure; and (3) *empowerment*, which involves giving clients the tools to combat racism in daily life. Within each phase, I describe the scientific literature behind each technique, along with guidance for applied practice of these techniques with clients. I also include verbatim examples of what therapists can say to clients as they navigate each phase of treatment.

It is important to appreciate that this protocol alone is not enough to make you an effective therapist for clients with racial stress and trauma. Treating racial stress and trauma requires you to be a culturally humble and empathetic clinician—qualities that are both learned. If you are doing this work, you need to embody an affirming presence, a deep well of empathy, and a big heart. Certainly, you would not be reading this book if you didn't care so much about helping people in pain. You also need to be aware of your own ethnocultural lens and racial biases, and you need to do your own work to make sure these biases are assessed and addressed. Any interventions for racial trauma must sit on a firm foundation of multicultural and racial competencies, and you must recognize racism's role in the cause of your clients' issues.

In this workbook, you will be asking clients to do some challenging things, so in addition to having the knowledge and attitude needed to be an anti-racist therapist, you should be able to do the things you are asking clients to do themselves. Much of the work clients will do, beyond processing their traumas, is learning a new way of approaching racism. This includes calling out microaggressions when they occur. As a therapist, you should ask yourself if you have ever called out racist incidents yourself. If not, you will need to make a concerted effort to not only increase your awareness of racist acts, but also build your courage to call them out in real time.

Treating people with racial stress and trauma is not easy, but it is important and vitally needed. You may wonder if you are the right person to do this work. But if not you, then who? Too many people of color suffer their whole lives with racial trauma, a condition that can be overcome with the right tools and the right therapist. You can be the change that is so desperately needed.

Foundations: Embodying an Anti-Racist Therapist

This workbook is intended for a broad audience, which means that you may be familiar with some of the information presented in this chapter. Even so, there may be new material, and a refresher can never hurt. Additionally, there are many beneficial exercises and reflections in this section worth repeating.

In chapter 1, you will:

- Review the basics of race, racism, and racial trauma.
- Develop an understanding of microaggressions and everyday racism, and the importance of being able to make a non-defensive repair of any cultural insensitivities committed in session.
- Explore personal ethnic and racial identity development, and understand how these dynamics impact the therapeutic relationship.
- Develop a working understanding of individualistic versus collectivistic cultural worldviews.
- Learn about being a racial justice ally, understand the difference between allyship and saviorship, and appreciate the importance of not being a savior.

Chapter Overview

Every therapist treating racial trauma needs to have several competencies, including the ability to identify and diagnose racial trauma, a willingness to discuss racism and cultural issues (even when it evokes discomfort), and an understanding of their own personal biases and blind spots that can affect the therapeutic relationship. Unfortunately, many current therapists graduated from clinical programs before they were required to receive multicultural training, and sadly some are still graduating today without such training (Benuto et al., 2019). Therefore, if you are not skilled or knowledgeable in these areas, you are not alone. Nonetheless, you will need to get up to speed and do your own work before attempting to treat racial trauma. To determine whether you are ready to provide safe and effective care to traumatized clients of color, reflect on your skills as a clinician. Here are a few questions you should ask yourself before you begin.

Self-Reflection Activity*

1. Have you had any formal training focused on multicultural counseling skills? If so, what type of training (graduate school, continuing education, etc.)?

2. Have you received clinical supervision from supervisors who are experienced in working with issues around race, ethnicity, and culture? If so, what did you learn from them?

3. Have you written case conceptualizations that have included considerations of your client's cultural identity and received feedback about your case from a knowledgeable supervisor?

4. Are you able to address racial differences with your clients of color consistently and early in the therapy process? What is an example of your approach, and how has your approach been helpful or harmful?

*Adapted from Williams, Faber, & Duniya (2022).

5. Are you comfortable asking, responding to, and supporting your clients with their experiences of racism and oppression? Are you comfortable and knowledgeable about intersectionality? What have been your challenges and successes?

____

____

____

____

6. Do you experience discomfort talking about White privilege and how the White experience is different in our society? If you identify as White, or White passing, can you identify 10 areas of privilege that you currently enjoy?

____

____

____

____

7. What is your familiarity with the current models of racial and ethnic identity development? Are you familiar enough to discuss how these factors might impact the therapeutic relationship with your clients of color?

____

____

____

____

8. When reflecting on your past and current caseload, how many consistent (i.e., at least 10 visits) clients of color have you seen? When reflecting on your retention of clients of color, are there any ways you may need to change to improve your numbers (if they are low)?

____

____

____

____

9. How would you respond if your client said you were a racist?

10. In your everyday environment, how well are you identifying racism? Thinking about a past or current workplace or school, what are (at least) five sources of structural racism you've noticed?

How did you do? How did this exercise feel? Did you feel equipped to answer the questions? If so, that is a great start! Or did you feel stumped or very uncomfortable? If so, don't despair; it's simply a sign that some focused work is needed, and doing that work will help you better serve clients from different cultural backgrounds. In this chapter, you will have a chance to learn more about some of these important issues.

What Are Racial Stress and Trauma?

Racial stress refers to the psychological response that an individual has to the experience of racism. Over time, these experiences can turn into *racial trauma*, which has been described as a psychological injury caused by hate or fear of a person due to their race, ethnicity, or skin color. But racial trauma is not just caused by the actions of a person filled with hate and fear. It is also caused by the systems of racism all around us. The cumulative nature of racial trauma eventually overwhelms a person's ability to cope and may emerge in many different ways.

Some Symptoms of Racial Stress and Trauma

- Feeling the world is unsafe
- Upsetting memories
- Anger and irritability
- Loss of trust in others
- Feeling emotionally numb
- Feeling one's life will be cut short
- Avoiding situations where microaggressions or racism might occur
- Often feeling on high alert
- Depression and sadness
- Difficulty sleeping or nightmares
- Guilt and shame

Diagnostically, some experiences of racial trauma, such as physical assault in the context of a hate crime, would meet the *DSM-5*'s criterion A for PTSD, which involves exposure to actual or threatened death, serious injury, or sexual violence. Other experiences—such as chronic exposure to microaggressions and secondhand trauma from seeing graphic coverage of police brutality—may not meet this criterion; however, these experiences are still considered a cause of racial trauma because previous research has shown that the prevalence and severity of PTSD symptoms are the same regardless of whether the traumatizing event meets criterion A (Anders et al., 2011). Racism can have the same devastating effects on BIPOC as discrete events like combat, sexual assault, or accidents that are recognized in the *DSM-5* as leading to severe mental and emotional injury.

Untreated racial stress may lead to the development of secondary disorders, too, such as major depressive disorder, substance use disorders, social anxiety disorder, and even psychosis. Though racism is linked to many mental health conditions, the connections between racial discrimination and PTSD symptoms seem to be the clearest. Most importantly, people with racial trauma experience individual psychological suffering, but the source of the problem is not within the person but, rather, the result of our dysfunctional Western society.

To think about how racial trauma and stress may affect your clients, consider the following scenario:

Image credit: © fizkes; iStock

How would you feel if your new client said this to you? Angry? Defensive? Confused? Why would a client say something like this? Is she wrong? Sadly, she is probably right. Studies have shown that Black clients are less likely to be offered appointments than White clients, even in places as diverse as New York City, and even when clients are part of the same insurance plan (Kugelmass, 2016). Working-class Black men have the hardest time getting even a callback, much less finding anyone willing to see them. In fact, Kugelmass (2016) showed that a working-class Black male client who needed an evening appointment would have to call 80 therapists to find one that was willing to see him! This shows that there is racism even among mental health professionals. As a result, your client may already be experiencing racial stress surrounding the treatment process before you have even said a word.

Understanding Racism

To understand racial trauma, it is important to learn more about race and racism itself. *Race* is a social caste system that assumes the superiority of one group over all others. We will discuss this more later in this chapter. *Racism* can be defined as a system of beliefs (racial prejudices), practices (racial discrimination), and policies (structural racism) based on race that benefit those with historical power—namely, White people in the US, Canada, and most other Western nations—and that disadvantage people of color. The term *people of color* refers to those of African, Asian, Latin, Indigenous, and Native American heritage and is meant to be inclusive of all non-White groups in the US and Canada, emphasizing the common experiences of racism. In contrast, the term *White* refers to people of European ancestry with light skin.

The following table outlines several different types of racism that people of color may experience.

Table 1.1 Some Different Types of Racism

Type of Racism	Definition
Dominative racism	This refers to the belief that there is a fundamental biological difference and superior intelligence over a racial group, making that group inferior. These types of beliefs allow for feelings of disgust and anger to be communicated without consequences from the harm they cause to the targeted person or group. This type of racism is also known as "old-fashioned racism," where racists explicitly act out biased beliefs (e.g., racial violence and racial slurs).
Symbolic/ modern racism	This type of racism involves harmful beliefs and negative stereotypes about people of color. Some refer to this as "right-wing racism." Examples include the belief that Black people no longer face prejudice or discrimination or that Black people's failures are because they're unwilling to work hard enough. This last example upholds the false idea that all people are afforded the same opportunities in society and denies the impact of systemic racism.
Aversive racism	This form of racism can sometimes be confusing to understand because people who demonstrate aversive racism are those who are outwardly supportive of racial equality. Because of this, aversive racism is also called "left-wing racism." Most commonly, people who are aversively racist are openly anti-racist, but they also have internal (and potentially unconscious) negative feelings toward people of color. You may have heard the term *unconscious bias*, which is another example of aversive racism. The intentions of people in this category are to be anti-racist, but they end up being racist in private or in uncertain situations.
Internalized racism	This type of racism occurs when people of color believe there are inherent differences between racialized groups. They may hold stereotypes about their own or other racial or ethnic groups (consciously or unconsciously) and collude to support systems of racial oppression. As such, they may experience self-hatred or negative ideas about other people of color. Other examples may be people of color who actively distance themselves from others in their own group or who prefer to spend time with or act like "White people," as they feel like it's better to be White.
Racial microaggressions	Microaggressions are small acts of racism that are less obvious and that are often committed by people outside of their awareness. Microaggressions can look like backhanded compliments or patronizing statements like "You are so articulate," which implies that it is unusual for someone of that race to be intelligent.
Structural racism	This refers to the development and upholding of policies, laws, and customs that benefit White people and give White people more power than other ethnoracial groups. An example would be government policies that perpetuate unfair lending practices for home buyers resulting in the denial of mortgage applications from people of color at a disproportionately higher rate than White people. Other examples include biased policing and laws that allow for voter suppression.
Systemic racism	All racism is, by definition, systemic. This means that it is a part of all our social systems, and these systems work to uphold all other types of racism.

Are these terms confusing? Learn more: Haeny, A., Holmes, S., & Williams, M. T. (2021). The need for shared nomenclature on racism and related terminology in psychology. *Perspectives on Psychological Science, 16*(5), 886–892. https://doi.org/10.1177/1745691621100076O

Awareness of Racism

Racism is a common occurrence, sometimes so common that we don't even notice it happening. Not only do we fail to see it, but we fail to act. Most people claim that if they were confronted with a situation where someone else said or did something racist, they would do something about it. But in reality, most people do nothing. This is why so many decades after the Civil Rights Movement, racism continues to be tolerated and keeps causing harm.

The purpose of this exercise is for you to determine your level of awareness and courage when it comes to racism and also to explore your areas for growth. For this activity, set aside some time in a space where you can focus and think about the last time you saw an act of racism. Choose something that happened over the last *two months*. It could be something that happened at your workplace or something inappropriate that a friend or acquaintance said. It could be something that someone you know posted about on social media. Then reflect on the following questions.

1. What was the incident and why was it racist?

____

____

____

2. How did you feel?

____

____

____

3. What did you do in response to the incident and why?

____

____

____

4. What could you have done differently?

____

____

____

How did you do? Did you show up the way you wanted to in the face of racism? Would people of color have called you an ally based on your behavior? How did your actions align with your values?

Understanding Microaggressions

Microaggressions are deniable or covert acts of racism that reinforce untrue stereotypes, social exclusion, and unfair treatment (Williams, 2020b). Microaggressions can take many forms and often include things that people might say or do, but they can even be environmental acts, such as naming an institution after someone who perpetrated racism. A couple of examples include the naming of "Strom Thurmond High School" in South Carolina, where Thurmond was a well-known proponent of racial segregation, and the statue of Egerton Ryerson, which was recently removed from the University of Toronto. Ryerson played a role in the creation of the Canadian Indian residential school system whose impact amounted to cultural genocide.

One microaggression that seldom gets much mention but may be overrepresented among therapists is called "connecting via stereotypes." This is when a person changes their speech or other behavior to try to seem more like the target so that they feel more alike and can better bond with them. Unfortunately, this usually causes just the opposite of the desired effect if the therapist's behavior change reflects a belief in racial stereotypes. An example of this would be a therapist who thinks that Black people prefer urban clothes, so he dresses down for his Black clients (e.g., Bergkamp et al., 2023). Rather than wearing his usual professional attire, which includes slacks and a tie, he wears a track suit and high-top sneakers. But rather than making his Black clients more comfortable, they perceive they are considered less valuable than the therapist's White clients because he does not bother to dress up for them.

Another example of a microaggression is when therapists make assumptions about a client's history based on what they believe their upbringing was like. For example, consider a therapist who assumes that because a female Muslim client of color wears a hijab, then she must have experienced oppression and sexism from her parents. As a result, the therapist might emphasize a need for empowerment when developing the client's treatment plan, failing to realize that this client's family encouraged her to have a meaningful professional career. Conversely, a therapist may assume an East Asian client was pressured by their family to focus on academic pursuits when this may not have been the case. Even if it were true, it may be offensive to the client that the therapist makes this assumption based on racial stereotypes. Table 1.2 provides further examples of microaggressions.

Table 1.2 Common Microaggressions

Theme	Examples	Message
Not a true citizen	▪ "What country are you from?" ▪ "Where are you really from?" ▪ "Where did you learn English?"	▪ The person being judged is not a real member of the community due to their race. Non-Whites are illegitimate citizens and must be immigrants because they're not White.
Racial categorization and sameness	▪ "What race are you?" ▪ "You don't look Native American."	▪ People of color must disclose their racial identity. ▪ People of a certain race are all the same and fit into one box. ▪ BIPOC must disconnect from their lived experience and ascribe to what they're "supposed" to be like.
Assumptions about intelligence, competence, or status	▪ Telling a Black person, "You're so articulate." ▪ Telling an Asian person, "You must be so good at math."	▪ It is unusual for certain people of color to be intelligent. People of color are not as intelligent as White people (with the exception of Asian people, who must be high achievers in math and the sciences).
False color blindness, invalidating racial or ethnic identity	▪ "I don't see color." ▪ "I only see one race, the human race."	▪ A person of color's experience of racism is untrue or invalid; their identity and cultural being is not significant. ▪ All races should acculturate to the dominant White culture.
Criminality or dangerousness	▪ When a store security guard follows around a customer of color. ▪ When a White person checks their wallet as a person of color passes. ▪ When someone walks across the street to avoid the person of color walking toward them.	▪ People of color are criminal, dangerous, and harmful.
Denial of individual racism	▪ "I have so many Black friends and Latino friends." ▪ "I'm a woman, so I know what it's like to experience discrimination." ▪ "I'm on the diversity, equity, and inclusion committee at work."	▪ Someone is immune to racism because of proximity to friends of color. ▪ Racial and gender oppression are the same. ▪ Past or current anti-racist work means that someone is never racist and that they are now immune to making mistakes and committing microaggressions.
Myth of meritocracy	▪ "Everyone can succeed if they just work hard enough."	▪ Everyone has an equal chance to rise to success and race is irrelevant to achieving success.

Theme	Examples	Message
Reverse-racism, hostility	▪ Denying that there is inequality in work access and opportunities. ▪ Stating that programs "unfairly" disadvantage White people. ▪ Expressing jealousy or hostility toward people of color for their supposed advantages.	▪ People of color receive unfair benefits because of their race or are undeserving of success.
Pathologizing minority culture or appearance	▪ Criticizing a person of color because of their appearance, traditions, behaviors, or preferences.	▪ Whiteness is the preferred and acceptable expression, while non-White identities are something negative or shameful.
Second-class citizen/ignored and invisible	▪ Giving a White person preferential treatment as a customer over a person of color.	▪ People of color are to be treated with less respect and care than is the expected norm in a situation.
Tokenism	▪ Using a Black person in marketing materials to give the impression of company diversity, when in reality, it is a majority White (or White-led) organization.	▪ It is acceptable to use others' racial identity to promote the illusion of inclusivity. People of color can be used as props.
Connecting via stereotypes	▪ Changing your appearance or behavior to match what you assume a person of color will relate to. ▪ Telling a racist joke to "fit in."	▪ White people can use stereotyped speech or behavior to be accepted or understood by a person or group of color. ▪ It is appropriate or entertaining to repeat racist stereotypes if it's all in good fun.
Exoticization and eroticization	▪ Characterizing a person of color as "exotic." ▪ Asking to touch a Black person's hair.	▪ It is okay to use sexualized stereotypes or perceived differences when interacting with or describing a person of color.
Avoidance and distancing	▪ Avoiding close relationships with people of color or discussions of race with people of color.	▪ People of color are to be avoided or actions must be taken to prevent physical interactions.
Environmental exclusion	▪ Excluding depictions of people of color in public art displays. ▪ Omitting literature representative of a non-White cultural identity.	▪ Only White people should be represented in public environments.
Environmental attacks	▪ Naming buildings after slave owners. ▪ Creating and maintaining Confederate monuments. ▪ Creating Columbus Day and upholding it as a federal government holiday.	▪ It's good to revere or celebrate people who have harmed people of color.

Importantly, many therapists can commit microaggressions against clients without realizing it. This can further any racial trauma that clients are experiencing, erode the client's trust in the therapist, and impede therapeutic progress. The example of Cassandra is presented here to illustrate how this can occur.

The clinician attempts to build rapport by engaging in small talk.
So, Cassandra, tell me a bit about yourself. How long have you been out of school?
Do you have a job?
Yeah, I have a university degree in international law. I'm currently working as a lawyer
at this big law firm and—

Image credit: Naomi Faber, used with permission

As Cassandra's example illustrates, even well-meaning therapists can erode rapport and further racial trauma when they make comments anchored in racial stereotypes, no matter how subtle. This is why it is so critically important to have knowledge of the unique false stereotypes about each ethnoracial group so that clinicians do not commit racist acts in the form of microaggressions.

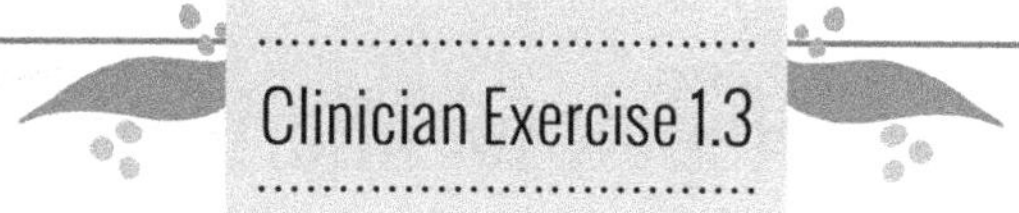

Awareness of Microaggressions

Microaggressions are common, and because they are the result of racist beliefs that are upheld in Western culture and that are internalized unconsciously, no one is immune from committing a microaggression. Moreover, microaggressions are often difficult to see, understand, and act upon, making it difficult to disrupt the pattern. To increase your awareness of these subtle forms of racism, think about the last time you committed a microaggression. Try to pick something that occurred recently (or if you cannot think of anything recent, then something in the last *12 months*), then reflect on the following questions.

1. What was the microaggression? If you're unsure, read through table 1.2 to review common microaggressions that happen.

2. After the microaggression happened, what were your thoughts and feelings? For example, were you aware that it was a microaggression? What did you notice about the other person's reaction?

3. What did you do and why? If you did nothing, say why.

4. What could you have done differently?

Rupture and Repair for Microaggressions

Even with strong clinical training, therapists will make mistakes in clinical practice. As clinicians, our experiences and biases enter the therapy room, impacting the language we use and the information we communicate—and this can lead us to unintentionally harm our clients in session. Whenever ruptures occur as a result of racism or cultural insensitivities, unintentional or not, it is important to be able to initiate repair with clients in a non-defensive way.

It's important to know that your client may not use the term *microaggression* when pointing out a rupture that has occurred. Instead, they may say that they felt like you were stereotyping, disrespecting, or misunderstanding them because of their racial, ethnic, gender, sexual, or other marginalized identity. Hearing from someone that you've committed a microaggression can make you feel shocked, hurt, embarrassed, defensive, or all of the above! It can be really hard to hear this from a client, especially when you've taken the time to carefully build a good relationship with them.

When these types of ruptures happen, it's an opportunity to continue to model what safe communication and repair look like. The following steps can help you move toward fixing a problem in this delicate situation.

1. Put the situation into perspective. Although you have been confronted with a problematic behavior witnessed by your client, this does not always mean your client feels you are a terrible person.	
DO: ▪ **Recognize that your client is most likely feeling hurt,** though they may seem like they're feeling angry, aloof, or distant. ▪ **Use this as an opportunity** to learn something about yourself and deepen security and trust in therapeutic relationships. A gentle initial response can go a long way toward defusing a delicate situation, such as: "Thank you for trusting me enough to bring this to my attention."	**DO NOT:** ▪ **Go into despair.** Appreciate that your client is coming from a marginalized identity and is trusting you enough to share this difficult information. ▪ **Tell the client they misunderstood you.** Hear them out fully before trying to explain yourself.
2. Avoid getting defensive. Making excuses for what you did is the biggest trap that you can fall into when a microaggression has been called out by your client. It may be true that you had good intentions and meant no harm, but it's not about intent—it's about impact.	
DO: ▪ **Agree there is a problem** to be addressed. Your client should be taken seriously, given that disclosures about microaggressions are uncomfortable and generally not communicated lightly. ▪ **Really listen to their concerns.** Do not interrupt. *Let the client talk first before you respond!*	**DO NOT:** ▪ **Attempt to provide evidence of your goodness** and prove that you aren't a bad person. Even if you're actively working against oppression most of the time, you may still do prejudiced things. The goal is not to never make mistakes but to understand that you may make them and be able to genuinely self-reflect and offer amends.

<table>
<tr><td>

- **Preemptively apologize** and show you care. You may say something like "I'm sorry. What I said was hurtful and insensitive. It is always my goal for you to feel safe around me. If I created an environment that made you feel hurt, that is a problem and I want to hear more so I can learn from it." Your client needs to know you are a caring person who is willing to be accountable, learn, and change, just as you are asking them to do in therapy.

</td><td>

- **Talk about your ancestry or other stigmatized identities.** No one is immune to committing microaggressions.
- **Attempt to teach the client about their own cultural history,** as this can be seen as patronizing or attempting to justify your behavior.

</td></tr>
<tr><td colspan="2">

3. **Ask for more information.** If you are not completely clear why your actions were wrong, ask your client while paying careful attention to what they have to say.

</td></tr>
<tr><td>

DO:

- **Communicate caring and openness** with your body language (e.g., arms open, not folded, body position relaxed).
- **Show humility.** Be okay with saying you don't understand. Ask, "Would you please explain more so I can better understand?"
- **Work to relieve the distress** you triggered and reestablish trust. For example, you may say, "I'm sorry you have had to deal with these painful things, and now here with me doing the same. You deserve better."
- **Validate the client's pain and frustration.** Make it clear you care about their pain.
- **Ask about and show sympathy for similar experiences your client has had.** Ask if they have experienced this behavior from you or others in the past. Express sympathy for past and current acts of prejudice, stereotyping, or intolerance your client is facing.

</td><td>

DO NOT:

- **Go into the conversation assuming the client is wrong,** especially if you are White, male, straight, affluent, and/or cisgender. People of marginalized identities identify microaggressions more accurately than people with advantages.

</td></tr>
<tr><td colspan="2">

4. **Acknowledge your biases and blind spots.** Many people have been desensitized to pathological stereotypes and do not realize these are false beliefs to begin with. Continually identifying biases is how we work to prevent committing microaggressions.

</td></tr>
<tr><td>

DO:

- **Consider your culture's history** and its relationship to the structural challenges working against equality.
- **Remind yourself that you are not exempt**—in Western culture, everyone is influenced by racism, sexism, homophobia, and other forms of discrimination.
- **Make a commitment** to continually acknowledge the unconscious, unwanted biases that still exist in you and commit to do better.

</td><td>

DO NOT:

- **Assume you know all of your blind spots,** even if you've had a lot of culturally responsive therapy training or are engaged in social justice and equity practices. Understanding your biases requires continually examining and questioning yourself and how you show up with your clients.
- **Villainize the client** for pointing out your microaggression. By doing so, you deflect attention away from your own error as a clinician who has a responsibility to ensure client safety.

</td></tr>
</table>

- **Ask, "Is there anything else I can do to make this right?"** Do not start here, though—starting with this question may make it look as if you don't want to make space to hear your client.
- **Be willing to experience discomfort.** This process can feel overwhelming and frightening to address as a therapist, but if addressed properly, it can strengthen your relationship with the client and serve as a corrective experience.
- **Over-apologize.** Once the issue has been addressed, do not keep checking in on how the client feels about you. Center the experience on what is best for your client. All they likely need is an acknowledgment and short apology. Over-apologizing puts your client in the position of emotional caretaker, where they are expected to soothe and heal you as the aggressor, which may discourage future disclosures because they worry you will not be able to handle it.

Learn more about racial microaggressions in therapy: Williams, M. T. (2020a). *Managing microaggressions: Addressing everyday racism in therapeutic spaces*. Oxford University Press.

Understanding Whiteness

In clinical practice, you may sometimes see White people who are suffering from racial trauma. You might be wondering if this means the person was mistreated by people of color. It is relatively rare for a White person to be traumatized as a result of being persecuted over their White identity (Carter et al., 2020). Additionally, the impact of racial stress on White people is not amplified by the same ongoing systemic racial oppression as it is for people of color. However, many White people who reject the unspoken rules of Whiteness may start to experience racial stressors. For example, White people who are racial justice activists may receive scorn from other White people who think such individuals are "race traitors."

People in racialized societies inherently expect White people to maintain the concept of Whiteness as the standard to compare all groups against—a standard that upholds the rule of better treatment for White people and worse treatment for people of color. As a result, White people who stand up to racism may be persecuted by their peers for doing so, which may result in traumatization. When White people experience mistreatment in connection to their race, it is a minority experience and something that they are less used to. Being rejected by one's own group can be particularly traumatizing and can act as a strong motivator to maintain the status quo, which explains why so few White people are willing to engage in the hard work of dismantling racism. It can be painful to resist long-standing racial norms and engage in racial justice allyship. This can even lead to racial trauma in White would-be allies.

Cultivating an Intersectional Lens

How you provide treatment for clients in clinical practice is deeply impacted by your own cultural experiences, so it is crucially important for all clinicians to consider how their own identity may be influencing and potentially limiting their approaches when working with people of color with racial trauma. Essential to providing the highest ethical standards of care is cultivating an *intersectional* lens. An intersectional lens is a viewpoint that accounts for the fact that all marginalized facets of a person's identity can interact to create a unique oppressive experience. For example, the way Black men experience racism can be very different from the way Black women experience it, and low-income people of color have a different lived reality than affluent people of color.

Traditional training programs too often do not help clinicians explore their personal ethnic and racial identity development and how that may present in the room with clients. A good place to start in this process is to take accountability for how your cultural background and relationship with power and privilege (or lack thereof) are present in the therapeutic relationship with each of your clients. You can begin to cultivate this intersectional lens by completing the following exercise.

Awareness of Power

Reflect on the following areas to gain a deeper understanding of your relationship to power and privilege and how that is impacting yourself and your clinical practices. Jot down a few sentences for each area listed below as it applies to you personally. What do you learn about yourself to help you in your work with clients based on your own positionality?

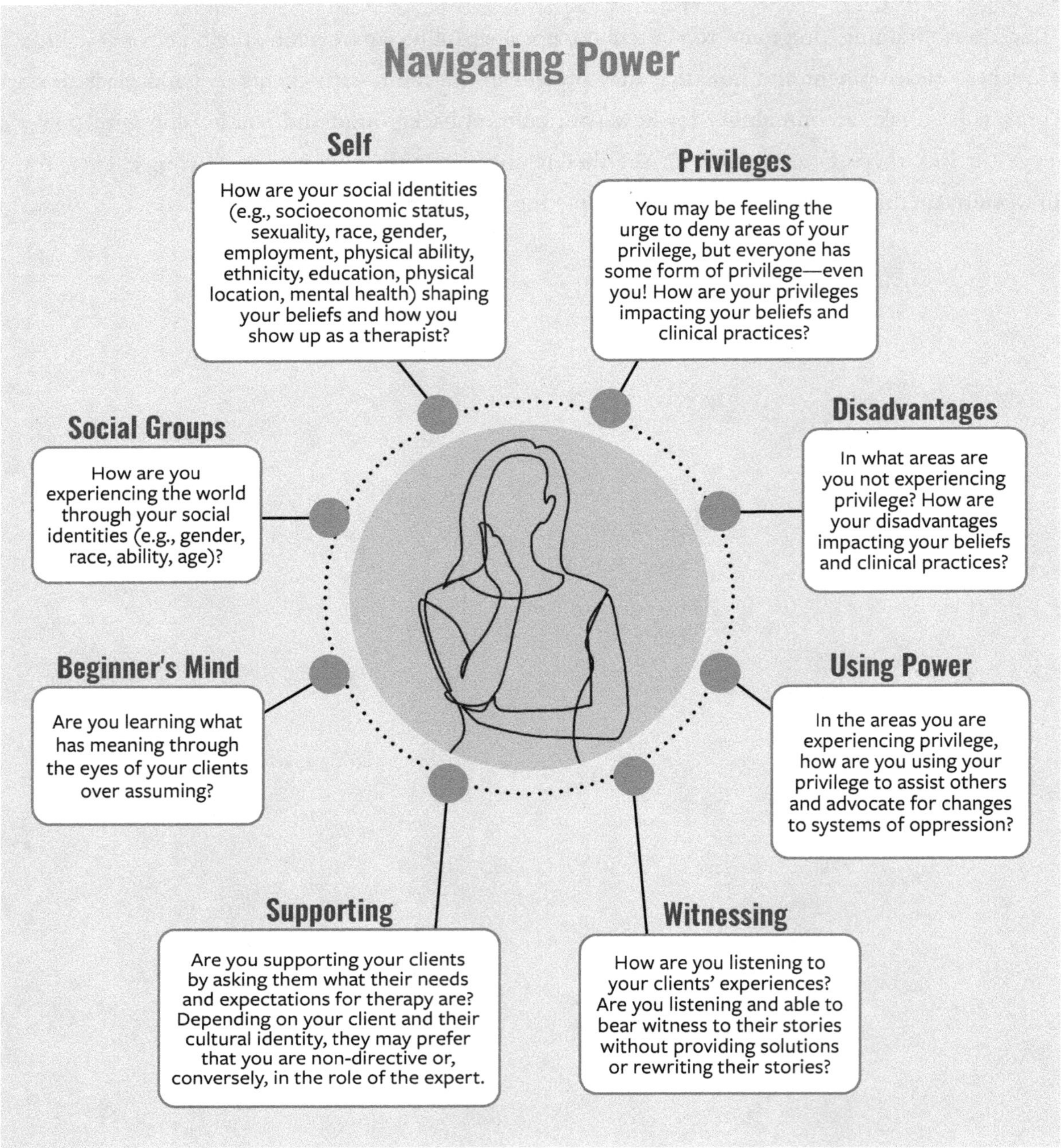

Navigating Power

Self

How are your social identities (e.g., socioeconomic status, sexuality, race, gender, employment, physical ability, ethnicity, education, physical location, mental health) shaping your beliefs and how you show up as a therapist?

Privileges

You may be feeling the urge to deny areas of your privilege, but everyone has some form of privilege—even you! How are your privileges impacting your beliefs and clinical practices?

Social Groups

How are you experiencing the world through your social identities (e.g., gender, race, ability, age)?

Disadvantages

In what areas are you not experiencing privilege? How are your disadvantages impacting your beliefs and clinical practices?

Beginner's Mind

Are you learning what has meaning through the eyes of your clients over assuming?

Using Power

In the areas you are experiencing privilege, how are you using your privilege to assist others and advocate for changes to systems of oppression?

Supporting

Are you supporting your clients by asking them what their needs and expectations for therapy are? Depending on your client and their cultural identity, they may prefer that you are non-directive or, conversely, in the role of the expert.

Witnessing

How are you listening to your clients' experiences? Are you listening and able to bear witness to their stories without providing solutions or rewriting their stories?

1. **Self.** How are your social identities (e.g., socioeconomic status, sexuality, race, gender, employment, physical ability, ethnicity, education, physical location, mental health) shaping your beliefs and how you show up as a therapist?

2. **Social groups.** How are you experiencing the world through your social identities?

3. **Beginner's mind.** In what ways are you approaching your clients to learn what has meaning through their eyes? In what ways are you assuming their experiences?

4. **Supporting.** How are you asking clients about their needs and expectations for therapy? Is your role as a therapist more directive or non-directive? You are the mental health expert, but your clients are the experts on their experiences—how do you balance this? How does your role as a therapist interact with your clients' cultural identities?

5. **Privileges.** How are your privileges impacting your beliefs and clinical practices?

6. **Disadvantages.** In what areas are you not experiencing privilege, and how are those areas impacting your clinical beliefs and practices?

7. **Using power.** In the areas you are experiencing privilege, how are you using your privilege to assist others and to advocate for changes to systems of oppression?

8. **Witnessing.** How are you listening to your clients' experiences? Are you listening to their stories by bearing witness, or are you listening and providing solutions or rewriting their stories?

Race Versus Ethnicity

Racial and ethnic identity development is the process by which people make sense of their race and ethnicity. Because race and ethnicity are such problematic concepts in our culture, it is a process that can be challenging for people of color and White people alike. However, understanding the distinction between ethnicity and race is important. Although there may be similarities and connections between the two, they are separate concepts.

Ethnicity can be thought of as the expression of one's cultural identity, or the process by which people understand and connect to their cultural background. When considering ethnic identity, we acknowledge the significance of traditions, customs, and emotions associated with our heritage. As we grow up, we go through various stages of development where we learn to connect with our culture. This involves gaining an understanding of our community's traditions and beliefs, allowing us to develop a sense of belonging to our ethnic group.

In contrast, *race* is about physical traits that lead to social categorizations based on stereotypes. This has led to the creation and continuation of systematic disparities. Race itself is an inherently racist concept by virtue of its deliberate placement of people into unfair castes and categories based on how they look and their assumed heritage. Race is a label assigned to us by others, while ethnicity is a label we choose for ourselves based on our cultural connections and social belonging. Ethnicity is a complex and multifaceted identity that encompasses both our actual heritage and the heritage we identify with.

Although race and ethnicity are both socially invented categories, they both have real-world implications that shape our identity. For example, while accepting and celebrating ethnic diversity can contribute to cultural richness, mutual understanding, and acceptance of other traditions and perspectives, race as a social construct has been used to build and sustain systems of power, privilege, and discrimination. The historical and present ramifications of race have resulted in socioeconomic inequality, marginalization, and injustices experienced by people of color.

Furthermore, ethnic identity is more inclusive compared to race, meaning that individuals of one race can identify with multiple ethnic backgrounds simultaneously. For instance, someone can be both Jewish and Black, Arab and White, or French Canadian and Asian. The ability to self-identify and have overlapping ethnic identities allows individuals to have agency in defining and expressing their sense of belonging and cultural heritage. This is in contrast to racialization, which is an external process that is imposed upon an individual (Williams et al., in press).

Table 1.3 Differences Between Race and Ethnicity

Race	Ethnicity
Arbitrary categorization: Individuals are classified into mutually exclusive categories based on skin shade and visual features.	**Self-identification:** Ethnicity reflects how individuals personally identify. It can encompass genetic, ancestral, cultural, historical, fluid, and overlapping factors.
Social construction for control: Race is a tool for establishing hierarchy and dividing populations. Invented and instrumentalized in times of colonialism and slavery, it leads to discrimination.	**Self-construct for culture:** Ethnicity encompasses shared cultural practices, traditions, and languages and can evolve over time due to migration, assimilation, or other societal changes.
External imposition: Individuals are subjected to racialization, where identity is imposed from the outside based on someone's appearance and presumed ancestry.	**Agency in definition:** Individuals define themselves and their identity based on culture. Ethnicity offers a more respectful approach, acknowledging more freedom to self-define.
Non-overlapping categories: Defined by governing bodies and based on public perceptions, these categories can change based on the needs of those in power.	**Diverse expression:** There are approximately 650 self-defined ethnic groups across 190 countries, demonstrating a rich diversity of human identity. Categories often overlap.
Genetic fallacies: Racialization is susceptible to attributing inaccurate traits based on perceived race.	**Genetics:** An individual's genetics may make up some or zero components of their ethnicity.

While ethnicity evolved for the well-being of specific groups of people, race is imposed by society. However, race and ethnicity are conflated in many societies, so people of color often relate to their racial group as well. For example, in the US, belonging to the African American ethnic group requires that a person be racialized as Black. Similarly, although Hispanic was once considered a racial group, it is currently considered an ethnic group—although many Latine* people do not identify with any race other than Latine or Hispanic. Therefore, throughout this manual, I often talk about a person's "ethnoracial" identity, which refers to the ways that someone may define themselves on the basis of their racial and/or ethnic identity. People may use many different terms to describe their ethnoracial identity. These terms may or may not match how these groups are defined by the government or in academic writings, but it is generally recommended to use whatever term the client prefers.

* The term *Latine* was created by LGBTQIA+ Spanish speakers. The letter *a* or *o* is replaced by the letter *e* to illustrate gender inclusivity within existing Spanish pronunciation. While *Latinx* is more common, some Indigenous people reject the use of the letter *x*, which colonists forced into languages during conquest and may be hard to pronounce by Spanish speakers (Guhlincozzi & Wallace, 2022).

Table 1.4 Current US and Canadian Government Racial Group Terminology

Canada		US
▪ White	▪ Arab	▪ White
▪ South Asian	▪ Southeast Asian	▪ Black or African American
▪ Chinese	▪ West Asian	▪ American Indian or Alaska Native
▪ Black	▪ Korean	▪ Asian
▪ Filipino	▪ Japanese	▪ Native Hawaiian or other Pacific Islander
▪ Latin American	▪ Other (specify)	▪ Some other race

Racial and Ethnic Identity Development

Identity Development in People of Color

How society categorizes ethnoracial identities may not seem to directly impact an individual's experience of their identity, but over the course of a lifetime, most people living in the US and Canada will have to continually categorize themselves using these terms, which can feel microaggressive and distressing over time. As individuals from marginalized ethnoracial groups come to understand themselves in relationship to their own culture and the more dominant culture at large, they typically go through five different stages of identity development (Atkinson et al., 1998; Sue & Sue, 2013). These stages represent the different attitudes and behaviors that a person of color might have as they work to accept and honor who they are as an individual (Williams et al., in press):

- **Conformity:** When a person of color values the majority cultural views, they are expressing conformity. When people are in this stage, they may feel negative emotions toward their identity. They may prefer White role models, believe it is better to be White, and value White standards of beauty and success. Example: A client rejects a same-race dating partner and views White partners as more desirable.

- **Dissonance:** An individual in this stage begins acknowledging the personal impact of racism. Events or triggers may be opening their eyes more clearly to racism, and they may begin examining and questioning their own set of beliefs, along with experiencing confusing and conflicting thoughts toward dominant cultural systems. Example: A client feels shocked after being harassed, threatened, and searched by police at a party on a college campus, while their White student friends are not bothered.

- **Resistance:** Here, the person actively rejects the dominant culture, and their individual involvement within it, because it is racist. They may even say they "hate" White people. Example: A client will not consider working with a culturally competent White therapist, even when no therapists of color are available.

- **Introspection:** The individual starts questioning their values both within their own ethnoracial group and as part of the dominant group. Example: A client joins a club espousing egalitarian values that has only White members.
- **Integrative awareness:** During this stage, a person's ethnoracial and dominant cultural values begin shaping their cultural identity. Additionally, they begin to experience more confidence and comfort with themselves and their identity with a desire to contribute to their larger society. Example: A client serves as a DJ at a White friend's wedding and plays favorite songs from mostly Black artists, which is in turn well received.

In your therapeutic work, it's important to recognize that many clients may not initially place significant emphasis on their race or ethnicity. However, over time, they will often come to realize that their experiences can markedly differ from those outside their racial or ethnic group. This realization leads them on a journey of self-discovery, where they actively decide what this aspect of their identity means to them. It's important to understand that as they develop a stronger and more positive ethnoracial identity, it can serve as a protective factor, helping to shield them from some of the detrimental effects of racism and bolstering their self-esteem. Supporting clients in this process of identity formation and affirmation can be key to fostering resilience and well-being in the face of racial challenges.

The following are some questions you can ask clients to better understand their ethnic or racial identity (Roberts et al., 1999; Williams, Metzger, et al., 2018):

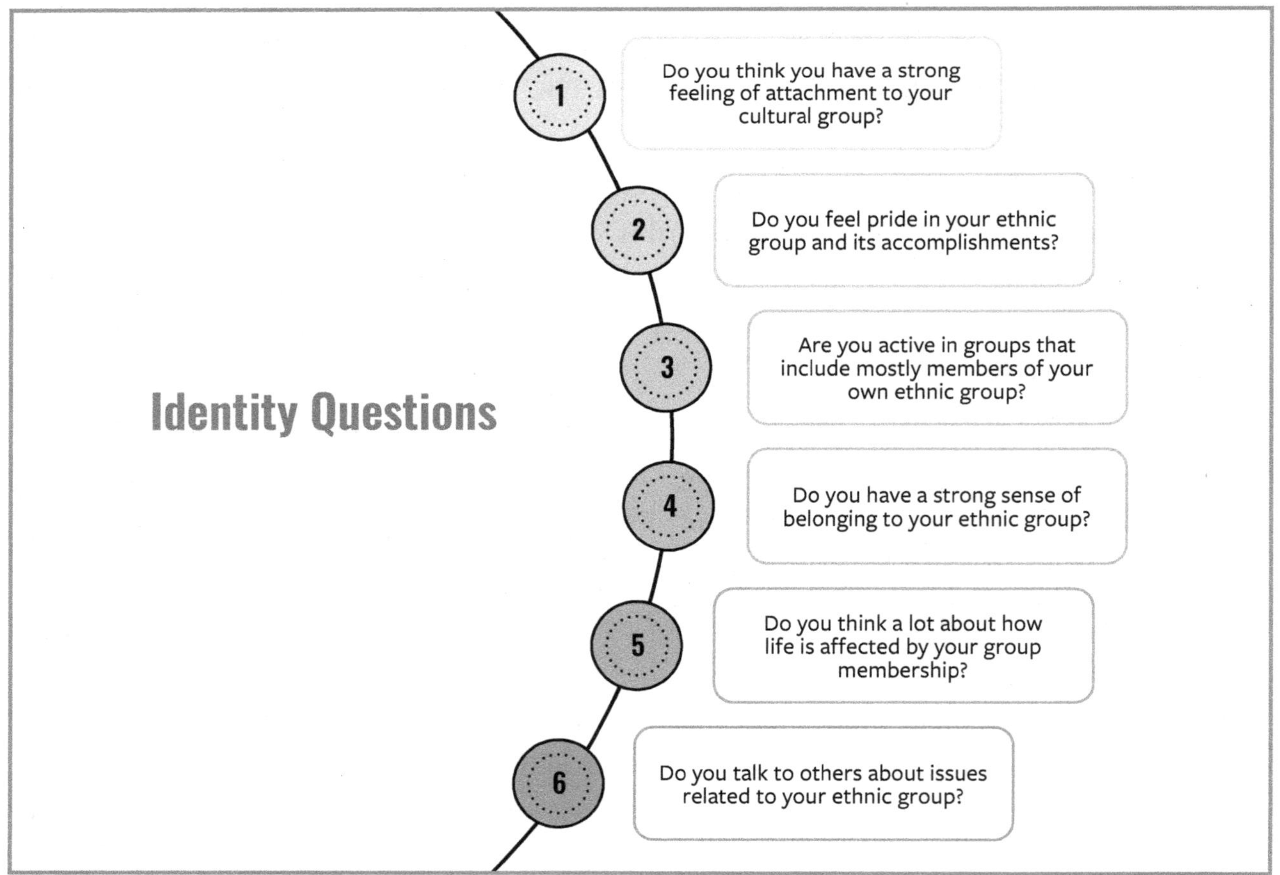

White Identity Development

Image credit: © Iakov Filimonov | Dreamstime.com

It is not just people of color who have an ethnoracial identity—White people do as well. However, most White people do not think about their own Whiteness, do not define themselves by skin color, and consequently experience themselves as non-racialized (Neville et al., 2001). They don't think about how their lives might differ from others due to their Whiteness. They also do not see how their Whiteness has given them power and privilege compared to people of color, especially if their own experience of their lives has included hard work and struggle. This can make developing a positive and prosocial White racial identity challenging, and it can make it difficult to understand the experience of people of color.

However, you must start to understand Whiteness as a race, privilege, and social construction, or you cannot shift into understanding what it means to be anti-racist. The idea that Whiteness is a racial identity was first introduced by Janet Helms, who created the White identity theory model to describe the process by which White people come to understand their own race and its relationship to racism (Helms, 1990). According to Helms, an individual moves through six different stages as they navigate this process (Williams et al., in press):

- **Contact:** An individual in this stage fails to acknowledge racial issues, which may be exemplified by their colorblindness or insensitivity to acts of racism. They may deny racism, cultural differences, or membership in the dominant group. Colorblindness upholds Whiteness as the standard measure and invalidates the distinct experiences that people have based on race. Example: A person says, "I don't see color; I just treat everyone the same" when racial topics are discussed.
- **Disintegration:** Here, the individual is conscious of their Whiteness, yet they experience a moral conflict when choosing between what is for the greater good of humanity and their own ethnic

group. Example: A person feels bad about being given a coveted job due to ingroup bias, even though a colleague of color was more qualified.

- **Reintegration:** A person in this stage experiences some understanding of their Whiteness and privilege, yet they continue to be intolerant or blame other ethnoracial groups. They may feel as if being White is wrong and transform this associated guilt into hostility toward people of color. Example: A person tells the Black people he meets at university that they only were admitted through affirmative action programs.
- **Pseudo-independence:** The individual decides to accept the truth of racial inequalities but with limitations. They may make efforts to connect with people of color but only those that are most similar to themselves or the dominant group. Example: A person notices that his golf club is all White and invites a fellow golfer who is Filipino to play one weekend.
- **Immersion/emersion:** Here, the individual understands White privilege more and works toward accepting its impact, though their actions may still be founded on feelings of guilt. Example: A person feels bad that the local cops arrested and tasered his elderly Black immigrant neighbor, so he leaves the neighbor flowers.
- **Autonomy:** At this final stage, the individual fully accepts their Whiteness and the continual learning processes necessary to understand the roles that they play in maintaining it. Additionally, they fully value diversity and feel far less fearful and guilty about the realities of racism. Example: A person sees White joggers calling the police on a group of Latine teenagers who were minding their own business in a park and stays to tell the officers it was all a mistake.

Appreciating White identity development can be difficult. White people in in our society live in a social environment that shields them from racial stress. Many are taught from a young age that they should not acknowledge racial differences, which includes differences in how people may be treated. This sheltered environment allows White people to forget that they are part of a racialized society and decreases their ability to consider or discuss racial issues. In order to have productive conversations about race, White therapists must be in a more advanced stage of ethnoracial identity development (i.e., immersion/emersion or autonomy) such that they feel comfortable discussing race, acknowledging their White privilege, and actively working to relinquish this privilege whenever possible.

If you want to have meaningful conversations around racial issues, you must also encourage growth among clients who are in the early stages of their own identity development, but you cannot help move the client further than you have come yourself. The best way to develop a strong, positive White identity is to forge meaningful friendships and connections with diverse people of color and to focus on becoming an excellent anti-racist ally, which is discussed later in this chapter.

Advancing Your Racial Identity Growth

The models just covered are very helpful for understanding identity processes but can also be considered just an outline of what it would really mean to transcend our racialized frameworks. Based on these models, what stage are you at in terms of your own racial identity development? How did you determine this? Would your friends of color agree?

Although it is easy to outwardly reject the morality of a dominant White culture, much work is needed to achieve an advanced identity status for a person of any race. Sometimes it can be helpful to visualize these steps to understand: (1) where society has been and (2) where society could be if we continue advocating for our systems to reflect not only racial diversity, but racial equity. In the following figure, reflect on the flow toward a society where diversity and community are valued.

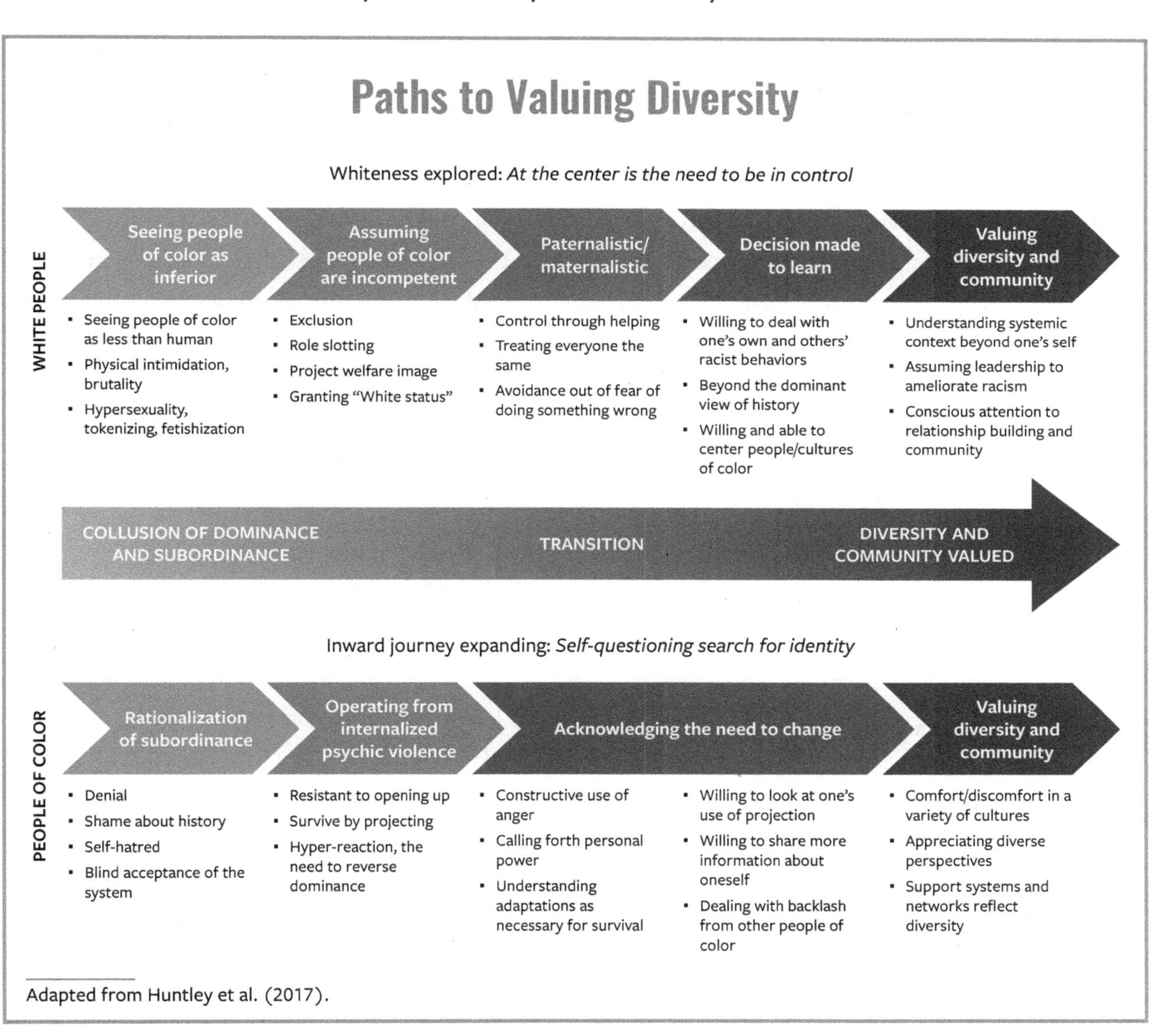

Adapted from Huntley et al. (2017).

Individualism Versus Collectivism

Individualistic cultures prioritize the autonomy and independence of individuals, emphasizing personal achievements, rights, and needs. In such cultures, people are often seen as separate entities, and the value is placed on self-expression, personal choice, and individual responsibility. The focus is on standing out and being unique, with success often measured by personal accomplishments. The dominant White culture in most Western nations, including the US and Canada, exemplifies individualism.

In contrast, *collectivistic* cultures emphasize the importance of groups and communities, such as families, workplaces, or nations. In these settings, people emphasize the needs and goals of the group as a whole over the needs and desires of each individual. Relationships with other members of their community and the interconnections between people are central to each person's identity. Collectivistic cultures value ways of doing things that are selfless and put community needs ahead of individual needs. Working as a group and supporting others is a critical social skill in collectivistic cultures. People are expected to do what is best for their communities, and family life is central to well-being. There are notable mental health benefits to collectivism, as individualism leads to more social isolation, placing people at greater risk of loneliness and suicide, and this may be particularly relevant for women and immigrants.

Most ethnic groups are collectivistic in their values and behaviors, and Black, Asian, Latine, and Indigenous communities each have shared histories rooted in interconnectedness and collectivism. The cultural worldviews of these communities emphasize the importance of connection as an aspect of psychological healing from oppression.

Examples of Common Collectivistic Practices

- Living in multigenerational households
- Showing obedience and respect toward elders
- Placing family needs over individual needs
- Helping others succeed
- Being humble and eschewing self-promotion
- Deflecting praise from the individual toward the group
- Emphasizing common goals over individual pursuits
- Favoring compromise when making group decisions
- Valuing generosity over self-interest

Learning how to heal racial trauma may require that you develop approaches to working with people of color that encompass different ways of being, where learning ancestral knowledge and cultivating social justice are key elements of healing. Collectivistic approaches allow space for racial healing, where authenticity and comradery are prioritized and where you can be part of the refuge needed to help shelter clients from ongoing racism. Here are some things you can say that will resonate with a collectivistic approach:

- *"We are all connected. When harm comes to you, it comes to me too. Racism harms all of us."*
- *"Because we are connected, your healing benefits all of us. When you become stronger as a* [e.g., mom, friend, and wife], *your kids get stronger, your relationships improve, your marriage heals. We all heal as a community."*
- *"I've used the harm I experienced to help others, and you will too."*

Taking a collectivistic approach to healing also requires that you take care when it comes to power imbalances in the therapeutic relationship. Some ethical principles of equitable healing for mental health professionals working with people of color include:

- Awareness of power dynamics in your relationships with clients of color
- Approaching clients of color in a way that is collaborative
- Consciously working to reduce racial power imbalances
- Recognizing the mutual benefits of the relationship
- Enjoying being in the presence of the client
- Appreciating that the client has put their trust in you as the therapist
- Valuing bearing witness to client stories

Racial Justice Allyship

What Is Allyship?

Allies are members of a dominant social group, or ingroup, who work toward fairness for people in a non-dominant group, or outgroup. Ingroup and outgroup terminology is drawn from social identity theory, which offers a helpful frame for considering intergroup dynamics, particularly when an ingroup, such as Whiteness, is defined through exclusionary practices. Allyship requires supporting non-dominant racial groups by having meaningful relationships with people in those groups and taking concrete action to make things fair. Allyship consists of both public and private behaviors that can include calling out discrimination, making space for voices of color, and fighting for inclusion of outgroup members. Here are some key points about racial justice allyship:

1. Allyship is about support, not leadership.
2. Allyship is a continuous process that cannot be "achieved," but to which one aspires.
3. One cannot self-prescribe the label "ally." It is a designation given by members of the non-dominant group with which one aspires to ally themselves.

Importantly, White allyship is a little different from other forms of allyship, such as LGBTQIA+ allyship, which was popularized by the ubiquitous "Safe Zone" programs that began in the 1990s. As part of that program, individuals were encouraged to use rainbow logos to self-declare themselves as visible allies to the LGBTQIA+ community. However, a person cannot proclaim themselves a White ally simply because they wish to adopt this label; rather, their efforts must first be recognized by people of color as exemplifying true allyship. (And even in the case of Safe Zones, queer and trans people still expected their allies to actively support the cause! [Williams, Sharif, et al., 2021]).

White Racial Justice Allies Are Those Who:

1. Have a good understanding of all forms of racism and White privilege
2. Engage in ongoing self-reflection about their own racism and place on the social hierarchy
3. Feel a sense of responsibility and commitment to using their racial privilege in ways that further fairness
4. Actively do things to stop racism in large and small ways
5. Build partnerships with people of color
6. Expect and experience resistance from other White people

Unfortunately, many people confuse White allyship with White saviorship, which involves engaging in acts of helping for personal benefit, self-image, or recognition. White saviors follow a charity model of help or have a paternalistic view of helping those they consider "less fortunate," all the while still feeling superior for being White and keeping social and emotional distance from people of color. Real allyship is about identifying and decentering Whiteness, empowering others even when this involves peer conflict, and creating space for reciprocal vulnerability. This may include discussing uncomfortable or shameful topics about race with others and disclosing shortcomings and missteps. It also means spending quality time with people of color outside of work hours. Allies ask BIPOC what they need and do it, whereas saviors make assumptions about what BIPOC need and take action based on their own comfort and notions of what they think is best.

For conscientious White people who aspire to be allies, the experience of Whiteness can be accompanied by guilt, shame, and helplessness. If this describes your experience, you can redefine what it means to be White. You may need to consider that certain traits or advantages that you consider negative aspects of your identity can become positives when used in the service of racial justice. For example, although White allyship is difficult at times, having a White identity gives you certain power in our society to bring attention, intervention, and justice to situations in which a person of color would not be able to act. You can choose, as part of your identity, to be a "shield of the oppressed" (see Williams, Faber et al., 2023). You can also look for opportunities to relinquish White privilege, such as listing "prefer not to answer" on certain forms where being White might be advantageous or allowing a person of color to go first in line at a store.

Learn more:

Williams, M. T., Sharif, N., Strauss, D., Gran-Ruaz, S., Bartlett, A., & Skinta, M. D. (2021). Unicorns, leprechauns, and White allies: Exploring the space between intent and action. *The Behavior Therapist, 44*(6), 272–281.

Liu, H. (2021). White allyship. In *Redeeming leadership: An anti-racist feminist intervention* (1st ed., pp. 141–156). Bristol University Press.

Confronting Racism

When it comes to tackling racism, White allies can use their privilege as part of the ingroup, playing an important role in helping to reduce incidents of individual or systemic racism against people of color. One way to do so is to confront racism in the workplace, where people of color, who may be less financially secure, are often the least able to take risks. Anyone who has union members in their family knows that many heroic people were willing to lay their jobs on the line in acts of civil courage that led to benefits for all working Americans. However, over the decades, there has been an erosion of community as more people tend to live rather insular lives, which has lowered the level of risk that people are willing to take on behalf of others. Yet as we spend so much time in the workplace, there are still things White allies can do to build civil courage that do not risk loss of livelihood.

One way to build civil courage is through the following exercise, which is intended to help you enhance your ability to confront racism and improve your skills as a racial justice ally. It is based off a recent article in *American Psychologist*, which introduces several CBT exercises to enhance racial justice allyship (Williams, Faber, et al., 2023). While this exercise might seem uncomfortable, remember that you will be asking your clients to learn new ways of relating to racism, and as a good CBT therapist, you must be able to do the exposures asked of your clients.

Confronting Racism*

Workplaces typically demonstrate racism in many forms—such as executive positions that comprise all White people, DEI committees that function as organizational window dressing, and HR departments that are more concerned about protecting the company than victims of workplace discrimination—which provides you many opportunities to show up as a White ally. The following are ways you can begin confronting racism in the workplace:

1. If you work in a mental health facility, ask your clinical director, "What specific actions do we take to make sure clients of color are having the same quality of care as White clients?"
2. If you work at a university, try finding an administrator or even a department chair, and ask, "What is our department doing to improve racial diversity among incoming graduate students?"
3. If you are part of an advantaged group, start demonstrating your support as an ally by asking those in less advantaged groups what their needs are to help bring new attention to issues and by venturing outside your comfort zone.
4. You can also ask whether salaries for position levels and counts of race per position can be made public, or ask about the gender and racial representation at the managerial and executive levels of a company. These are polite ways to challenge the workplace status quo.
5. If you're hearing or witnessing racist behavior, simply repeating back the offensive comment to the speaker may be enough to alert them of their negative impact.
6. If the previous alerting strategy is not enough, you can also begin explaining how the comment landed and ask if the speaker intended it to be hurtful or unsettling to the other person (e.g., "What you said made me feel very uncomfortable. Those comments are rooted in ignorance, and I wanted you to know that").

Do not be surprised if your racially privileged friends or colleagues react to your actions by taking offense or becoming embarrassed. When you encounter these types of reactions, you might feel like backing away, but acting in accordance with your true values as a White ally makes room for healthier, caring, and respectful relationships. Taking even a small risk can be a source of tension, but you can strengthen your resilience and your resolve by continuing to willingly expose yourself to such stressors, which can also be a way to produce growth.

* Adapted from Williams, Faber, et al. (2023).

Build your capacity to confront racism: Williams, M. T., Faber, S. C., Nepton, A., & Ching, T. H. W. (2023). Racial justice allyship requires civil courage: Behavioral prescription for moral growth and change. *American Psychologist, 78*(1), 1–19. https://doi.org/10.1037/amp0000940

Can White People Treat Racial Trauma?

Ethnic matching in therapy has been shown to improve the therapeutic alliance and decrease dropout rates, so clients may think that therapy will be more effective if they are matched with a therapist who has an innate understanding of their culture. Indeed, given the benefits of working with someone from the same ethnic group, it may seem like the best way for clients to feel comfortable. It is natural for people to prefer talking about their experiences of racism with someone of the same ethnic or racial background, and the therapist may provide more accurate information about the client's symptoms.

However, ethnic matching in the treatment of racial trauma is not always possible because there are not enough therapists of color to meet the needs of all clients of color. The reality is that systemic barriers in higher education keep many people of color out of mental health professions. Additionally, a client of color may actually prefer someone who is *not* a part of their own ethnic group for a number of reasons. For example, they may struggle following their cultural group's norms and, in turn, worry about judgment from someone from their same community. Or they may be at an early stage of their ethnoracial identity development, leading them to idealize White people and therefore prefer a White therapist.

Unmatched dyads are not always a bad thing. When a person of color works with a White therapist, this can be an opportunity for both people to grow in awareness, connection, and cross-cultural understanding. It might be helpful to note that White clients can also grow from having a therapist of color. And people of color may grow from working with a person of color from a different ethnic group. But for this to occur, it requires that the therapist operate from a culturally informed and anti-racist framework.

Some clients may express that they feel unsafe working with a White person since they associate White people with the racial trauma they experienced. Do not lose heart if clients tell you this! If you are White, the fact that they are sitting with you means they are open to this possibility, and the fact that they are sharing this means they have trusted you enough to be open with their concern. They are just hoping you will be different from others who have harmed them. If they express concerns that show they have misgivings, you can say the following:

> *"Thank you for sharing this with me. I am really glad you are willing and able to advocate for your own emotional safety in this process. Would you share more about what has made you feel unsafe around White people (or White clinicians)? I would like to understand your perspective and experiences so that I can do better than those who have mistreated you or left you feeling unsafe. I will do my very best to make this a safe space for you, and if I ever fall short, I want you to let me know so I can learn from it and make things right between us."*

Here are some other things you can say, depending on your therapeutic style and the needs of the client:

- *"I appreciate your honesty and courage—that you have left your safe space to come to see me, a White therapist, when you don't have any reason to trust White people. I am deeply honored that you are giving me this chance to help you."*
- *"White people in our society are socialized to maintain racism, whether or not they are aware of it. So it would be prudent to be wary of any White person who has not done their own anti-racism work. There are not many, so it would make sense not to trust."*
- *"Your feelings are valid, and they point to a history of bad experiences that have caused you to have this mistrust. It makes sense."*

Above all, you want to connect with your clients and demonstrate that you will provide them with an affirming space in which you are validating, nonjudgmental, interested, genuine, receptive, mindful, and self-aware. You must be ready to acknowledge the role of racism and the importance of culture, be willing to grow and learn, and be able to advocate for others who are marginalized. One framework that can help you adopt this mindset is functional analytic psychotherapy (FAP), which is an approach that focuses on the therapeutic relationship as the key agent for change. In the next section, I will discuss the FAP approach in more detail.

Caring Affirmations

Clients with different ethnic or racial backgrounds to your own may have names that are unfamiliar to you. Make sure to take the time to learn how to pronounce the client's name, as well as ask for and respect their personal pronouns. If the client has a different first language than your own, you may even learn how to say key phrases in their mother tongue.

Connecting with Clients Through Functional Analytic Psychotherapy

FAP is similar to many CBT interventions in that it focuses on concrete behavioral changes and includes tasks for the client to practice outside of session, but it differs with respect to the amount of time and attention given to building a strong therapeutic relationship that will serve as the primary conduit for change. Within the FAP approach, the therapeutic relationship is a real relationship. This relationship is powerful in promoting learning and growth, motivating clients, and keeping clients invested in the therapy process. FAP also involves frequent checking in with clients to see how the approaches are working for them and to get them more tuned into how they feel about another person (you) in the moment. The key principles of FAP are awareness, courage, and love.

An FAP approach is particularly useful when working with clients who have experienced racial trauma, who may feel guarded and afraid to connect too deeply with others. FAP therapists can help clients learn to take the interpersonal risks that are necessary to cultivate strong relationships by experiencing, processing, and disclosing their own reactions to the client immediately as they occur in the session. When the client engages in courageous self-expression in session, the therapist responds with genuine heartfelt feedback to increase the connection through the exchange. This vulnerability and immediacy serve as a model that helps the client improve their connections with others. In this way, FAP supplements other CBT techniques such as psychoeducation, cognitive restructuring, behavioral experiments, and exposure. In fact, you can think of FAP exchanges as a type of interpersonal exposure.

You will notice FAP-based approaches in many of the examples I provide in this manual, especially in terms of ways of speaking or relating to the client. When clients have been harmed by racism, they are coping with feeling excluded and unloved. You will connect better with your clients if you can embody the opposite of that experience. Finding opportunities to affirm them as human beings, to praise them for their courage, and to join with them in their pain will accelerate the healing. Many clients feel shame over being victimized by racism, and FAP is one of the most powerful techniques we know of to melt away shame. You do not have to be an expert in FAP to provide the healing racial trauma protocol to clients, but if you know some FAP, it will help.

For example, imagine that a clinician is working with a Black woman who feels ashamed for being unable to cope with ongoing criticism and insults from her boss, who even insults her at staff meetings in front of her colleagues. She has developed anxiety that starts when she leaves her home each morning and is having trouble talking about the experiences because she thinks she is a weak person who should have been able to handle this abuse and cope better. The therapist might respond in this way:

> *"It makes perfect sense that you are feeling like this after dealing with this abuse, day in and day out. It really takes a lot to keep coming back to that workplace, not knowing what your boss will do, but knowing it will be bad. Thank you for trusting me with this. I can relate, at least in a small way, to how difficult it can be to face that kind of treatment from someone in authority. When I was in college, I had a professor who used to make fun of me in front of the whole class, and I felt powerless and humiliated. I just stopped going to class. So I don't know how you keep going back. When I look at you, I see a lot of strength."*

As a therapist, you appreciate that therapy is not about centering you and your experiences. However, you are a key part of the process, so you do need to show up as a real human being for FAP to work. If you are a White therapist, you will not know the pain of racism firsthand, but you can understand the pain of being excluded, humiliated, and misunderstood. You can share this where applicable. Too many White therapists make inadequate comparisons to their own experiences based on an incomplete appreciation of the pain of racism. This will always fall flat. You will need to dig deep to find a similarly painful experience to share. That being said, you should only share personal experiences that you have already processed.

Learn more about FAP: Tsai, M., Kohlenberg, R. J., Kanter, J. W., Kohlenberg, B., Follette, W. C., & Callaghan, G. M. (2009). *A guide to functional analytic psychotherapy: Awareness, courage, love, and behaviorism*. Springer Science + Business Media. https://doi.org/10.1007/978-0-387-09787-9

Conclusion

Hopefully after reaching this point, you have a greater understanding of race, racism, racial trauma, microaggressions, repair, and racial justice allyship. You also hopefully understand your own ethnic and racial identities and how these identities and power dynamics show up in your therapeutic relationships with clients. Understanding this foundational chapter will be key to moving forward through the rest of the workbook, so feel free to review or repeat these exercises at any point if you find yourself needing a refresher. Many of these exercises will uncover new things to learn about yourself each time!

Planning for Treatment and Assessment

This chapter will provide an overview of the healing racial trauma protocol and guide therapists in the use of clinical interviews and questionnaires that can screen for racial trauma and track improvements.

In chapter 2, you will:

- Learn specifics of the healing racial trauma protocol.
- Review how racial trauma relates to psychiatric diagnoses, such as PTSD.
- Explore effective measures to assess racial trauma.

Treatment Overview

As discussed earlier, the healing racial trauma protocol provides a series of guided sessions, each 60 minutes in length, designed to take place over a 12-week period. The protocol begins with an initial assessment for racial trauma, followed by three treatment phases: (1) stabilization and support, (2) healing, and (3) empowerment. Phase 1 focuses on getting highly distressed clients the support they need for stabilization—so much so that this phase is also referred to as "stop the bleeding." Phase 2 focuses on the use of cognitive restructuring and exposure exercises to help clients process their pain. Finally, phase 3 is about providing clients with practices they can use to combat racism in their daily lives for sustained wellness.

This protocol was developed and tested based on a peer-reviewed article published in the journal *Cognitive and Behavioral Practice* (Williams, Holmes, et al., 2023). It bears some similarities to other approaches for racial trauma, including the three-stage approach proposed by Herman (2015)—safety and stabilization, remembrance and mourning, reconnection and integration—while building on the racial trauma recovery approach developed by Comas-Díaz (2016) and the concept of radical healing proposed by French and colleagues (2020). This workbook will guide you through each step of treatment. Although the techniques are listed in roughly the order they should be used, certain techniques will be used throughout, and some may need repeating or periodic revisiting, depending on the client's progress and life circumstances.

Table 2.1 Healing Racial Trauma Treatment Overview

Phase	Goal	Techniques
Assessment	Understand the scope of the client's racial stress and trauma	Use of validated scales and clinical interview to assess racial stress and trauma
Part 1: Stabilization and Support		
Session 1: Making Sense of Racism	Reduce shame by helping the client understand that racism is caused by society and is not the client's fault	Psychoeducation about racism and resulting harms
Session 2: Coping and Self-Care	Increase functional strategies and decrease dysfunctional ones	Assessment of coping and self-care strategies (and a discussion of these with the client); promotion of self-compassion
Session 3: Cultivating a Support Network	Reduce stress and provide resources for when racial stress occurs	Identification of existing social supports and finding ways to create more
Part 2: Healing		
Session 4: Dismantling Internalized Racism	Reduce shame and increase feelings of belongingness	Cognitive defusion and restructuring; cultural exploration/appreciation
Session 5: Understanding Colorism and Building Ethnoracial Identity	Increase feelings of control by better predicting racism in the environment	Psychoeducation about race, including the invisibility of Whiteness
Sessions 6 and 7: Exposure and Processing of Experiences of Racism (*repeat as needed*)	Habituate trauma response through exposure; learn new thinking about the event; reduce distress, shame, and guilt	Conversations about distressing events; expressive writing; Socratic questioning; artistic expression
Session 8: Learning Strategies to Combat Racism	Build skills to respond to racism in various situations; increase confidence to act	Journaling of racist events to discuss in session; review of possible responses; role-play
Part 3: Empowerment		
Session 9: Combating Racism in Everyday Life (*repeat as needed*)	Increase feelings of agency toward racism; reduce feelings of helplessness and victimization	Graduated in vivo exposure to respond to racism in daily life; practice making predictions and processing outcomes; skill building
Session 10: Posttraumatic Growth and Meaning-Making	Recognize and reinforce success; engage in ongoing meaning-making of prior trauma	Consolidation of events into a cohesive and meaningful narrative
Session 11: Social Action and Activism	Promote change in the client's environment; promote feelings of agency	Evaluation of values; exposure to challenging situations; promotion of racial justice goals
Session 12: Goodbyes and Moving On	Facilitate relapse prevention; provide closure to therapy	Synthesize course of treatment and mastery of techniques

These strategies must also be considered in the context of their limitations. It is important to realize that the effects of oppression may have destabilized the client's life in many areas, making regular meetings challenging, so throughout the treatment process and especially in the beginning, you should be as flexible as possible (e.g., scheduling evening appointment times, providing phone or email support as needed).

Therapist reading: Williams, M., Faber, S. C., & Duniya, C. (2022). Being an anti-racist clinician. *The Cognitive Behaviour Therapist, 15*, Article e19. https://doi.org/10.1017/S1754470X22000162

Client reading: Williams, M. T. (2018, December 31). Demanding diversity: Tolerance is not enough. Psychology Today. https://www.psychologytoday.com/us/blog/culturally-speaking/201812/demanding-diversity-tolerance-is-not-enough

Assessing Racial Trauma

People of color experience regular acts of racism. Traumatizing events may include police searches and assaults, incarceration, workplace discrimination and harassment, and hate crimes. Refugees and immigrants may also have been victimized by ethnic cleansing and persecution, torture, and migratory hazards. It is important to explicitly ask your clients about these potentially traumatic experiences during the assessment because they may not volunteer all of this information out of shame or because some of the experiences are so common to them that they do not think of them as "traumas." Further, because so many people of color are used to their experiences being dismissed or invalidated, they may fail to mention their racial stress and trauma entirely.

Table 2.2 Common Sources of Trauma for People of Color

People of color may have trauma due to:	Immigrants and refugees may have trauma due to:	Other common sources of trauma:
▪ Racism and discrimination ▪ Workplace threats or harassment ▪ Racial profiling ▪ Assault by law enforcement ▪ Urban or gang violence ▪ Incarceration ▪ Abusive pregnancy and childbirth experiences ▪ Poor medical care	▪ Ethnic cleansing and persecution ▪ Experiencing or witnessing torture ▪ Living in a war zone ▪ Immigration difficulties ▪ Deportation ▪ Forced separation from family members ▪ Persecution of cultural practices or language	▪ Military service ▪ Motor vehicle accidents ▪ Fire or natural disasters ▪ Domestic violence ▪ Physical or sexual abuse ▪ Robbery ▪ Life-threatening medical conditions and procedures

That is why a racial trauma–focused assessment is so critical. This type of assessment takes into account the client's cultural background and unique experiences with racism or intersectional discrimination, allowing you to get the best picture of their symptoms, mental health history, and current life situation. This is particularly important given that racism and discrimination can lead to many mental health issues, including depression, anxiety, PTSD, and substance use. Identifying these symptoms through a comprehensive assessment will provide a more holistic picture of the client's difficulties, allowing for more targeted interventions that address the underlying causes of trauma. Most importantly, it allows for more client-centered care, providing clients with a chance to express their concerns in detail and feel more involved in their own care decisions.

If you attempt to use assessment measures that do not account for the client's experiences with oppression, you increase the potential for bias in the assessment process. For example, you may inadvertently use language or ask questions that contain hints of racism by being insensitive to cultural differences, leading to inaccurate diagnoses and ineffective treatment plans. Additionally, people of color experience more stigma when seeking mental health services, so creating a safe and supportive environment during the assessment sessions is of the utmost importance. Finally, many standardized psychological assessments lack the sensitivity needed to adequately identify experiences of racism or discrimination-related stress and trauma.

For these reasons, it is important that clinicians use culturally sensitive methods and tests when working with clients who have experienced racism and discrimination. By using validated assessment tools, you are ensuring an accurate diagnosis, confirming the appropriateness of the treatment plan, and making sure the best approaches for your clients are provided. This chapter outlines several practical tools that you can use. In addition to using these specialized tools, you should explore the centrality of the event to the client—that is, the degree to which the client feels that the event has become a core part of their identity. You can further ask the client what they believe the incident and the aftermath tell them about themselves.

Here is a recommended reading for clients to orient them to what you will be doing next in terms of the assessment and subsequent treatment. It tells the story of Amy, a 21-year-old Japanese American college student who was assaulted by racial slurs, and the steps her therapist took to assess Amy's race-related distress and develop a subsequent treatment plan. Providing reading such as this can ease clients into the habit of doing outside learning and preparing them for the work ahead.

Client reading: Williams, M. T. (2019, January 19). Uncovering the trauma of racism: New tools for clinicians. *Psychology Today*. https://www.psychologytoday.com/us/blog/culturally-speaking/201901/uncovering-the-trauma-racism-new-tools-clinicians

Collecting Basic Information

Taking a complete trauma history is necessary when assessing racial stress and trauma, as all traumas are cumulative, even those unrelated to racism. To begin, you will want to collect basic demographic information about your client. Sometimes, therapists struggle to figure out the best way to capture this information from their clients. Traditional demographic forms often do not provide a great picture of how a client's cultural background and experiences may inform their current mental health challenges.

Although it may feel unnecessary or even intrusive when collecting demographic information from clients, you should always ask about their race and ethnicity. Take some time to review your intake materials to ensure the language is current, accurate, and inclusive. Be sure to offer a write-in option that says "not listed; please describe" for all questions that allow participants to self-define, as the available options may not fit their identity. Asking a client to fill out a form with checkboxes that do not include an important part of their identity or experience can be off-putting. It can make clients feel like your clinic does not understand or value who they are, and it may affect attitudes toward treatment. As clinicians, we want to do our best to avoid contributing to clients' feelings of marginalization, and that experience can happen as early as the paperwork they are asked to complete (Williams, 2020a). In the appendix of this book, you'll find a culturally informed demographics form that you can use as part of this process (Suyemoto et al., 2016; Williams, 2020a).

Self-Report Questionnaires

When creating your treatment toolbox, you should administer self-report questionnaires to gather information about how your client is experiencing racial trauma and to track their progress. You may approach the subject by saying something like:

> *"To track your progress, it may be useful to have you fill out a couple forms at the beginning of our time together, and at several checkpoints throughout your treatment journey. These forms shouldn't take more than 15 minutes."*

You can then introduce the Trauma Symptoms of Discrimination Scale (TSDS) or the Racial Trauma Scale (RTS) to determine the severity of the client's racial trauma and their main difficulties. You should also administer the Racial Microaggression Scale (RMAS), along with any of the additional measures listed, as applicable. It is recommended that your client complete these as homework before the interview assessment.

Trauma Symptoms of Discrimination Scale

Though PTSD symptoms are varied, one of the most common symptoms is anxiety, which is often described as feelings of worry, nervousness, or discomfort around an upcoming situation that may feel uncertain or negative. In terms of discrimination, people with racial trauma may experience anxiety over where harm may come from (e.g., "Is that person a racist?"), physical symptoms (e.g., heart pounding), worries about losing control, self-doubt, or feelings that the other shoe is always about to drop. When someone is trying to ward off these uncomfortable thoughts and feelings associated with anxiety, avoidance is often the main coping strategy, which can lead them to socially isolate, dissociate from their own experiences, or engage in substance use.

To account for these symptoms, the Trauma Symptoms of Discrimination Scale (TSDS; Williams, Printz, & DeLapp, 2018) was developed as a measure of distress from discrimination, focusing on anxiety-related trauma symptoms and avoidance of fears of discrimination. The TSDS was initially tested in African Americans, where it was compared to several known measures of psychopathology and experiences of racism, including PTSD symptoms, traumatic cognitions, and racial trauma. The scale was found to have excellent reliability and has since been used in many studies and further validated in additional ethnoracial groups (Williams, Osman, & Hyon, 2023).

Research using the TSDS with diverse adults has shown that people exhibit more trauma symptoms when they experience more recent and past experiences of discrimination and more racial microaggressions, indicating that both overt and subtle acts of racism contribute to traumatization (Williams, Osman, & Hyon, 2023). This same research determined that oppression in all its forms is traumatizing, with some dimensions of oppression being more traumatizing than others based on a client's intersecting identities. For example, non-White Hispanic and Black Americans reported the highest rates of trauma symptoms, followed by Asian Americans and White Hispanic Americans. Additionally, sexual minorities were at significantly increased risk for trauma symptoms as a result of discrimination, as were individuals with three or more stigmatized identities (Williams, Osman, & Hyon, 2023). With this in mind, the TSDS allows clinicians to more closely consider all of these issues in clinical practice, individually and in combination.

The TSDS has two parts: The first part measures the frequency of experiences of discrimination, whereas the second part determines the types of discrimination experienced. A cutoff score of 40 indicates likely racial trauma. Working through part 2 of the TSDS provides opportunities for clients to gain a deeper understanding of how the aspects of their identities are impacting their experiences of discrimination and their relationships with the world around them; for example, clients may be able to see how one aspect of their identity is seen as more valued than another. You can find a copy of the TSDS in the appendix.

Racial Trauma Scale

The Racial Trauma Scale (RTS; Williams, Osman, et al., 2022) is a 30-item questionnaire that asks clients about their traumatic symptoms due to racial trauma. Clients are instructed to think about all the times they have heard about, seen, or experienced racial discrimination and to then rate the extent to which they are bothered by any associated thoughts, behaviors, or symptoms (where 1 = "not at all" and 4 = "extremely"). There is no time frame specified in the questionnaire, but clinicians can add their own time frame based on the needs of the assessment. For example: "As a result of this experience, how bothered have you been by the following *over the last two weeks.*" Higher scores are indicative of greater distress, with a clinical cutoff score of 48.

The RTS was developed for and tested with diverse ethnic and racial groups. It has been found to be highly related with other measures of trauma and stress, including the PTSD Checklist for the *DSM-5* and the General Ethnic Discrimination Scale. Developed in our own lab, the Williams, Osman, et al. (2022) paper featuring the RTS won the American Psychological Association's award for the top-downloaded journal article published in *Practice Innovations* for 2022. You can use this measure to zoom in on specific racial trauma symptoms in need of intervention and also track progress throughout the course of treatment by administering the RTS regularly. You can find a copy of the RTS in the appendix.

Racial Microaggressions Scale

Since microaggressions are detrimental to the mental health of people of color, it is important for therapists to know the impact of these chronic stressors. The Racial Microaggressions Scale (RMAS; Torres-Harding et al., 2012) is a measure you can give clients to assess the frequency of microaggressions they have experienced as well as the accompanying distress caused by these experiences. This allows you to measure the perceived stressfulness of microaggression experiences, creating a fuller picture of the impact of these events on your clients. The subscales on the RMAS divide microaggressions into the following six categories.

Table 2.3 Categories of Microaggressions on the RMAS

Category	Scale Definition
Invisibility	Being treated as if you are of lower status, not visible, or not seen as a "real" person; being dismissed or devalued
Criminality	Being treated as if you are aggressive, dangerous, or a criminal
Low-achieving/ undesirable culture	Being treated as if people from your racial group are interchangeable, uniformly incompetent, incapable, low achieving, and dysfunctional, and as if successes are due to unfair entitlements and special treatment
Sexualization	Being treated in an overly sexual manner and subject to sexual stereotypes
Foreigner/not belonging	Being made to feel as if you are not a "true" citizen/member of your society or do not really belong because of your race
Environmental invalidations	Negative perceptions that arise when you observe that people from your racial background are largely absent from work, school, or community settings or from positions of power

Semi-Structured Interview for Racial Trauma

The University of Ottawa Racial/Ethnic Stress and Trauma Survey (UnRESTS; a newer version of the original scale developed by Williams, Metzger, et al., 2018) is a semi-structured interview that you will administer before starting treatment to evaluate the impact of multiple experiences of racism over a client's lifetime (e.g., personal trauma, vicarious trauma, microaggressions). The UnRESTS is separated into six sections to learn about the important details of racism in a client's life, assess their formation of an ethnoracial identity, and probe for various racism-related experiences:

1. An introduction to the interview
2. Racial and ethnic identity development
3. Experiences of direct overt racism
4. Experiences of racism by loved ones
5. Experiences of vicarious racism
6. Experiences of covert racism (e.g., microaggressions)

It also includes a checklist of yes/no items to help establish whether the individual's racial trauma satisfies the *DSM-5* criteria for PTSD (29 items). This measure has been tested and adapted for use in Spanish- and French-speaking populations, including Canadians of color (Williams, Metzger, et al., 2018; Williams, Cénat, et al., 2024). The process of recounting traumatic experiences of racism can be quite stressful for clients, and they may feel distress for some time after the interview. After giving the interview, instruct the client to take it easy for the rest of the day, engage in relaxing activities, and spend time with supportive people as needed. You can find a copy of the UnRESTS in the appendix.

Learn more about racial trauma as PTSD: Williams, M. T., Ching, T. H. W., Printz, D. M. B., & Wetterneck, C. T. (2018). Assessing PTSD in ethnic and racial minorities: Trauma and racial trauma. *Directions in Psychiatry, 38*(3), 179–196.

Other Useful Clinical Tools

There are several additional measures that you can use to help understand a client's experiences more broadly. Some popular favorites are listed here.

Self-Report Measures

- **Beck Depression Inventory** (BDI-II; Beck et al., 1996): This widely used 21-item self-report inventory measures the severity of depression in adolescents and adults. Important to note is that the BDI-II is widely used as an *indicator* of the severity of depression rather than a tool to diagnose depression. Another benefit of this questionnaire is that it has been shown to be valid across different populations and cultural groups and has been used in many studies with trauma-exposed individuals. Since racial trauma can cause depression and even suicidal thoughts, this is a good way to check on the severity of symptoms in your clients, especially considering its proven validity across diverse populations.
- **General Ethnic Discrimination Scale** (GEDS; Landrine et al., 2006): This 18-item measure asks questions about unfair treatment across different environments (e.g., school, work) and situations

(e.g., bullying) as well as throughout the client's life (from childhood to the present). The GEDS takes around 10 minutes to complete and can be used across all racial identities. This measure is very helpful for identifying in which domains clients are experiencing most of their discrimination and how stressful it has been. This can then aid in designing treatment interventions, tracking progress, and providing focused treatment.

- **Multigroup Ethnic Identity Measure** (MEIM-12; Roberts et al., 1999): This is a 12-item measure evaluating the role of ethnic identity for youth and adults. It presents statements like "I have spent time trying to find out more about my ethnic group, such as its history, traditions, and customs" and "I have a strong sense of belonging to my own ethnic group," with items rated on a 4-point scale (1 = "strongly disagree" through 4 = "strongly agree"). This is a good way to help understand how connected clients feel with their ethnic group, as low scores can be an indicator of internalized racism.
- **Posttraumatic Diagnostic Scale for *DSM-5*** (PDS-5; Foa, McLean, Zang, Zhong, Powers, et al., 2016): This 24-item self-report measure assesses how severe PTSD symptoms have been for clients in the past month in relation to the *DSM-5* criteria for PTSD. The PDS-5 starts with two screening questions to assess trauma history and identify an index trauma, then follows with an item for each of the 20 *DSM-5* PTSD symptoms. An additional four items ask about distress and interference caused by PTSD symptoms as well as when the symptoms started and how long the symptoms have been present. Items are rated on a 5-point scale of frequency and severity ranging from 0 ("not at all") to 4 ("6 or more times a week/severe"). The PDS-5 is a valuable assessment tool for helping therapists understand the severity of a client's trauma-related distress. This can help you best tailor therapeutic interventions and monitor treatment progress over time.
- **Life Events Checklist for *DSM-5*** (LEC-5; Weathers et al., 2013): This is a self-report measure designed to screen for traumatic events across a client's lifetime, assessing exposure to 16 events known to potentially result in PTSD or distress, as well as one additional item accounting for any other extraordinarily stressful event not captured in the first 16 items. This checklist doesn't include specific items about racial trauma, but it can still be used as a beginning point to discuss a client's other traumatic experiences and examine any links to racial trauma experiences.
- **Posttraumatic Cognitions Inventory** (PTCI; Foa et al., 1999): This measure identifies trauma-related thoughts and beliefs. The PTCI items were derived from clinical observations and current theories of post-trauma psychopathology and look at three factors: negative cognitions about self, negative cognitions about the world, and self-blame. It is a useful measure to differentiate between traumatized individuals with and without PTSD, which can help identify clients who have PTSD but are reluctant to disclose mental health difficulties.
- **The Race-Based Traumatic Stress Symptom Scale—Short Form** (RBTSSS-SF; Carter & Pieterse, 2020): This is a 22-item self-report measure designed to assess the emotional reactions of racism and racial discrimination through seven subscales: depression, anger, physical reactions, avoidance, intrusion, hypervigilance/arousal, and low self-esteem. It involves a fairly complicated scoring process

but provides a separate score for each scale and can help provide a good idea of key areas in need of intervention. It is also available in an interview format.

- **Coping with Discrimination Scale** (CDS; Wei et al., 2010): This scale is used to assess how individuals respond to experiences of discrimination. More specifically, it evaluates the use of five coping mechanisms in relation to discrimination: detachment, internalization, drug and alcohol use, resistance, and education/advocacy. Because the CDS assesses how people of color cope with multiple forms of discrimination, it may be especially valuable for clients with intersectional identities, such as women of color and people of color who experience religious and/or sexual marginalization. It can help you to better understand where to support clients in their coping efforts and where changes may be needed.
- **Oppression-Based Traumatic Stress Inventory** (OBTSI; Holmes et al., 2023): This is a self-report measure modeled after the UnRESTS that uses the *DSM-5* criteria to assess for PTSD. It assesses for a range of discriminatory experiences in addition to racism, and it also solicits information about racism experienced vicariously (e.g., in the media) and by loved ones. Part A comprises open-ended questions asking clients to describe experiences of oppression and a set of questions to determine whether criterion A for PTSD is met. Part B assesses specific symptoms anchored to the previously described experiences of oppression and also asks clients to identify the various types of discrimination they have experienced. It is available free online.*

Clinical Interviews

- **Mini International Neuropsychiatric Interview** (MINI; Sheehan et al., 1997): This brief structured diagnostic interview assesses the 17 most common disorders in mental health as they are defined in the *DSM-5* and *ICD-10*. The disorders were selected based on those with current prevalence rates of 0.5 percent or higher in the general population in epidemiology studies. This measure is also useful for clinical settings where psychotic disorders are a concern and where it is important to differentiate between disorders that may include psychosis (e.g., PTSD vs. major depressive disorder). This is a good basic assessment to ensure no major areas of concern are missed.
- **Diagnostic Interview for Anxiety, Mood, and OCD and Related Neuropsychiatric Disorders** (DIAMOND; Tolin et al., 2018): This is a measure you can use with adult clients when there is a known or suspected mental health issue related to mood, anxiety, obsessive-compulsive disorder, or other related conditions. It contains diagnostic information for disorders that commonly co-occur with these conditions as well. It is important to note that this measure does not address all *DSM-5* diagnoses in those sections, so other assessments should be used if other mental health conditions are suspected. This is a free measure and very good at capturing anxiety-related conditions.

---

* You can find the OBTSI in the Supplementary Material section at the following website: https://www.frontiersin.org/articles/10.3389/fpsyg.2023.1232561/full.

- **Clinician-Administered PTSD Scale for *DSM-5*** (CAPS-5; Weathers et al., 2018): This 30-item structured interview is widely used to assess whether clients meet diagnostic criteria for PTSD. It assesses the 20 *DSM-5* PTSD symptoms and allows you to determine when the symptoms began, how long the symptoms have been present, the client's subjective experience of distress, and the impact of their symptoms on social and job functioning. The CAPS-5 can be used to assess the presence of PTSD symptoms during the current month, the client's lifetime, or the past week. It can also be used on an ongoing basis to track improvement in symptoms.
- **PTSD Symptom Scale Interview for *DSM-5*** (PSSI-5; Foa, McLean, Zang, Zhong, Rauch, et al., 2016): This is a 24-item semi-structured interview to determine whether the client meets the *DSM-5* criteria for PTSD in the past month. It begins by screening the client for *DSM-5* criterion A items and identifies if multiple events leading to PTSD have occurred for the client. It also measures the frequency and intensity of PTSD symptoms, with an additional four items asking about distress and interference caused by PTSD symptoms.
- **Cultural Formulation Interview** (CFI; APA, 2013): This is surely one of the best kept secrets of the *DSM-5*! Therapists may use this free interview to better understand the client's lived experiences, as it supports the therapist in learning more about the cultural definition of the problem, cultural perceptions of causes, cultural factors affecting self-coping and help seeking, and more. The CFI does not have questions that are specific to experiences of racism and oppression, but it can help provide a broader picture of the client's cultural context.

Providing an Assessment Report

After you have completed a thorough assessment of your client's symptoms, mental health history, and current life situation, you will want to share what you have found with your client, which can be done through a conversation or more formally with a report detailing your findings. Sometimes clients need documentation of their racial trauma for employers, worker's compensation, legal actions, or other official purposes. You can administer the interviews and questionnaires described here to help create valid reports for all of these purposes, if you otherwise have experience working in those contexts. If you have not created reports for legal purposes, you can do so in consultation with an experienced psychologist. All measures listed are validated and described in the peer-reviewed literature, so they can bolster interview findings and help substantiate mental health diagnoses, such as PTSD, major depressive disorder, social anxiety disorder, and other sequelae.

Conclusion

Using varying tools for assessment, like those discussed in this chapter, will be important to ensure that the process of diagnosis and treatment planning are aligned with your client's needs, and they will help you provide care from a culturally responsive lens. As previously mentioned, many standardized psychological assessments lack the sensitivity necessary to identify experiences of racism or discrimination-related stress and trauma, so using more culturally sensitive methods and tests is essential to capture your clients' experiences more fully. Additionally, the use of both guided and self-report assessments creates opportunities to build rapport with your clients and center their experiences when creating a plan for care, and moving forward, they provide a baseline to track each client's progress.

Now that the assessment phase of the healing racial trauma protocol is complete, you can move on to the first phase of treatment.

CHAPTER 3

Part 1—Stop the Bleeding: Stabilization and Support

Most clients with racial trauma have suffered for a long time and are coming for help now because they feel they are finally at their breaking point. This chapter will focus on stabilizing and supporting the client to start them on their healing journey.

In chapter 3, you will:

- Help your client understand the nature of racism.
- Review and strengthen coping strategies.
- Build your client's support network.

Chapter Overview

Those experiencing racial trauma are forced to exist in an environment that continues to perpetuate and add traumatic experiences of racism. To start the healing process, your client must first understand the wide-reaching effects of racism and its connection with the racial trauma (and related conditions) they are experiencing. That is the focus of this chapter, which is divided into three parts, with each part representing a weekly therapy session.

Session 1 is focused on making sense of racism and its many ripple effects. Subsequent sessions aim to help the client better surround themselves with the supports needed for the difficult healing work ahead. This includes learning about healthy ways of coping and actively practicing self-care, which is the focus of session 2, as well as assembling a strong support network, which is explored in session 3. However, don't get stuck on the idea that you have to finish each session in one clock-hour. Some clients may need more time and others less. This is just a guide.

When you first meet with a client, there may be some uncertainty about how to describe the healing racial trauma protocol. Here is one way you can approach this at the start of the treatment process:

> *"The purpose of this program is to help you heal from racial trauma. We will start by working together to understand exactly how racism can affect mental and emotional well-being. Together,*

> *we will process your painful experiences and learn new and effective ways to respond to all forms of racism you may encounter.*
>
> *"We will go over a different topic every week, and there will be some homework and exercises for you to do, like journaling how you tend to respond when someone does something racist. This may also involve you reflecting on things like automatic self-talk when something goes wrong.*
>
> *"We will discuss how to make sense of racism, negative beliefs about ourselves that can develop as a result of racism, and the connection between racism and trauma. It won't be easy, but it will be worth it."*

If you are White and have not already done so, this is a good place to acknowledge your White privilege by providing examples of unearned advantages you've received due to your race. White clinicians can voice that they aim to be non-defensive, want to avoid White saviorism, and demonstrate allyship and reciprocity. A key thing to keep in mind is that people of color do not need you or other White people to save them; they have the ability to advance but often face barriers to accessing resources to help them do so. With this in mind, focus on building your client's confidence in their abilities and help by jointly problem-solving barriers to achieving their goals.

> *"I know it can be difficult to be a person of color in our society today. People make a lot of judgments based strictly on how you look. As a White person, I do not get judged in the same way as you do. Others may make snap decisions about me due to my gender or other aspects of my appearance, but my race is never a problem in my everyday life. So, I realize that we have some really different daily experiences from that fact alone. I do get many advantages from being White, and my hope is that I can use that in service of creating a fairer world for everyone."*

Even if you are not White and are of a different racial or ethnic group from the client, it will also be important for you to speak about your ethnoracial differences transparently and with humility from the get-go. This may include acknowledging areas for growth and identifying steps you plan to take to learn more about your client's ethnoracial group so you can be most effective during treatment. This will help build trust by showing that you are willing to learn about the client's culture. This may be the first time anyone has made the effort to do so, which will be an important step in creating a culturally corrective experience. You are modeling the type of cross-racial relationship you want your client to be able to cultivate with diverse others outside of therapy.

As part of this discussion, encourage the client to share any concerns they may have about working with a therapist who is ethnoracially different, as well as concerns about counseling in general. Your role is to validate and better understand the client's experience—not to question the details of the situation or the severity of its impact. Further, encouraging the client to talk about ethnoracial differences is an important skill you will need to build with the client to later confront others who may not be as nurturing as you are. This is a baby step in learning how to have productive interracial dialogues—a common source of anxiety for many, especially those with racial trauma.

Session 1: Making Sense of Racism

A main purpose of this session is to use validation and psychoeducation about racism and its resulting harms to reduce shame and help clients understand that racism is not their fault.

Step 1: Validation

When clients are suffering from racial stress and trauma, validating their experience is essential. Validation includes acknowledging and exploring racist experiences and racism-related stress, normalizing these experiences and reactions, recognizing a client's strengths, and pointing out the resilience and coping strategies they have used in dealing with racism. As a rule, you should accept that all experiences of racism shared by a client are real and not imagined or exaggerated. Racism, by nature, is a system of social collusion that undermines the credibility and authority of those who experience it. A socially punishing response can make victims question their reality and pressure them into remaining silent and helpless in the face of ongoing abuse. For this reason, you should avoid the use of Socratic questioning around the accuracy of experiences of racism at this point, as it will only compound a client's confusion and shame. The most important initial step on the journey of healing is ensuring that clients feel seen and heard.

As you begin treatment, it is important that survivors of racial trauma are able to acknowledge their racialized experiences as racist events. For some, this acknowledgment may be straightforward and easy, but others might need help conquering denial, avoidance, and minimization. How you respond to a client's disclosures of racism is a crucial factor in the healing process. Racism is a challenging subject to work with, even for therapists who have been taught to be validating and supportive. Although you might be tempted to attribute a client's experiences with racist behaviors to other sources, you must be capable of validating the role that racism plays in the client's life, even in circumstances where you may question this perspective. Remember that it is possible to validate a client's perspective without necessarily agreeing with it. That being said, in my experience, clients are often ashamed of having been victims of racism, so they are much more likely to *understate* the impact of racism than the reverse. Their guilt and shame can arise due to self-blame and a misplaced sense of responsibility for the experience.

You can start to validate your client's experiences of racism through body language that expresses empathy (e.g., nodding thoughtfully, making empathetic facial expressions). Make sure to also verbalize support when the client discusses the reasons they sought treatment and the ways in which they have been harmed due to racism. You can offer responses such as "I am so sorry you had to experience that" or "Nobody should ever have to put up with those behaviors." You can underscore that racism is not the fault of the client by making statements like "That wasn't right for them to make you feel responsible for their prejudice." This may be particularly challenging for a therapist if the client describes being mistreated by people who are part of the same ethnoracial group as the therapist. If this is your situation, you must take care not to become defensive or assume the client is including you in this description.

Thoughtful Validation of Experiences of Racism

You can validate client experiences by repeating back what they shared and showing empathy for their reactions to the event:

> *"I was thinking about the story you shared during our assessment, when every time you applied for a promotion, it was turned down, and each time they gave a different reason. That is a good example of how racism operates to make people feel confused, less worthy than others, and off balance. It sounded like you were told that if you worked harder, you'd get that promotion, but you worked harder, and really all that happened is that you provided extra labor for your employer that was not compensated or recognized. And that is confusing. You'd said it was confusing because you worked so much harder and it didn't get recognized, but I also heard that you were working tremendously hard before your boss ever made that comment. So I think that had to be part of your confusion too."*

Step 2: Intensive Detox

In many cases, clients have internalized negative thoughts about themselves and their ethnic group that may contribute to the manifestation of psychopathology. This internalization often occurs because racism is built into the fabric of our society, so people of color are immersed in a toxic social environment day in and day out that attacks their self-esteem. As a result, they might develop some mistaken beliefs or falsehoods about themselves, including thoughts that they are:

- Not worthy
- Not smart
- Not strong enough or weak
- Invisible
- Unlovable
- Unattractive
- Incapable of achieving their goals

Because clients have made it a habit of thinking about themselves in this way, they hold these thoughts as true even though they are false and maladaptive. To counteract damaging negativity coming from all directions, an intense detoxifying experience may be necessary, which involves repeated affirming and positive statements about the client as a human being and their ethnic group. You can start by sharing that the field of psychology acknowledges the presence of false, mistaken, and unhelpful beliefs that are informed by racism but are simply untrue and are maladaptive. For example:

> *"You may believe these thoughts because you have made it a habit of thinking of yourself in this way, but these thoughts are not true or even helpful."*

The goal is then to be a corrective mirror, wherein you use emotional, empathic responses to reflect positive qualities in the client that they cannot see in themselves. Provide validating responses based on what the client has shared and be genuine (e.g., "Can I share what I've learned getting to know you? I think you're courageous, brave, funny, etc.")—and say how you arrived at those conclusions.

As you better understand how your client developed these negative beliefs about themselves, you will be able to genuinely validate your client's experience. For example, "The fact that no one else in your community has pursued a higher education must have made the idea of pursuing college feel like an impossible task. Would you agree?" or "It seems to me that being teased for having darker skin has made you feel unlovable."

This work will also involve pointing out evidence countering these negative beliefs. For example: "The fact that you received a full scholarship shows that you have what it takes to be successful in college" or "The fact that friends and family threw you a surprise birthday party and celebrated with you shows that you have many people who love and care for you." This disconfirming evidence will start to slowly erode away distorted thinking and shame over perceived shortcomings and failures.

Coming to important realizations like this will take time, so don't expect the client to understand and accept everything just yet. The emphasis at this point should be on providing supportive statements about the client's ethnoracial group to help strengthen their ethnic and racial identity, whether or not they are ready to take it all in. For example, in the case of the client who says, "I am sorry, but I just don't see any of these qualities in myself," you can say:

> *"That is all right. You've taken in a lot of toxins from our society that is polluted with racism. It is going to take time for us to rid you of that so you can see yourself the way you really are. We are going to work together on this. In the meantime, I will keep reminding you of how strong and talented you are when you forget until you stop forgetting."*

Many therapists are worried about being offensive—so they completely avoid talking about race, ethnicity, and culture. But supportive and positive statements about a person's culture can be an important means of helping them feel understood. You don't want to miss an opportunity to be supportive out of fear of offending. At the same time, it is important to make sure you are not promoting a racial stereotype. You want to provide caring affirmations that actively counter stereotypes. Comments should point to beneficial things the client does, such as spending time with family, volunteering, engaging in self-care, and so on, while taking care to avoid microaggressions.

Examples of Supportive Statements That Therapists May Avoid

- "Your cultural identity is a vital part of who you are, and I appreciate that About you."
- "I understand that there are unique challenges that come with being an Indigenous person, and I'm impressed with how you've managed those."
- "I appreciate your willingness to be vulnerable and share your experiences of racism with me. It takes a lot of courage to do so, and I want to acknowledge that."
- "What's it like being a Black person in your workplace? I want to understand that better."

Learn more: Abdulrehman, R. (2024). *Developing anti-racist cultural competence*. Hogrefe Publishing.

Step 3: Making Sense of Racism

Providing psychoeducation about the nature of racism to your client early in the treatment process is critical for building a foundation for healing. These concepts will be referenced and used throughout treatment, and they give clients a language with which to describe and process their experiences. Psychoeducation should not be provided as a lecture; try to make it as conversational as possible. A helpful start to this process involves asking your client to share their understanding of racism and its impact. This will give you a sense of the client's understanding and identify any gaps in knowledge.

Furthermore, you should spend some time teaching your client that experiences of racism are a social problem that makes their life more difficult in many ways and that brings about unmerited mistreatment, even if they are doing everything "right." Clients often have the common misconception that if they do the "right thing," they won't be harmed by racism. This might include following the rules, getting a good education, turning the other cheek, working hard, and being kind to everyone. People who think this way might be more likely to internalize or blame themselves when they experience racism. It is important to help your client understand the insidiousness of racism so that they properly externalize these experiences as opposed to internalizing them. The reality is that even when people do the "right thing," they can still suffer from the effects of racism. Helping your client understand this truth can shift their focus from simply doing what they always considered the "right thing" to engaging in behaviors that are consistent with their goals and values when they experience racism.

Deepening the Conversation About Racism

Use your client's experiences as a springboard for psychoeducation. Here are some examples:

- Name specific racist experiences the client's ethnoracial group has endured, such as colonialism and slavery, to encourage them to openly bring up racism-related topics during the course of therapy. For example, consider a 35-year-old client who is applying for a job as an instructor:

  "It can be challenging to enter academia as an Indigenous person. Prejudice and racism against Indigenous peoples stem from colonial beliefs that Indigenous peoples were weak, unworthy of care, incapable, savage, and primitive. Your life is likely still impacted by colonialism today. Even if you work harder than your colleagues, you may feel as if you are not on the same level as them. However, you have demonstrated that you are not defined by colonialism. I can clearly see that you are capable, intelligent, and effective in your role."

- Help your client understand where their negative self-beliefs came from and start challenging them in a supportive way:

  "It can be difficult to imagine succeeding beyond what people in your community have accomplished because there have been few role models on how to do so. Our society promotes the myth of meritocracy that successful people are able to 'pull themselves up by their bootstraps' and achieve their goals. This leads to the assumption that something is wrong with those who do not succeed—that they are lazy or inherently incapable. However, the reality is that not everyone has equal opportunity or access to resources to achieve their goals. Your community has faced structural barriers due to racism that have made it especially difficult for them to pursue their career goals. Despite these barriers, I can see that your family has instilled in you a strong work ethic, and that work ethic is what helped you obtain a full scholarship to college and will help you achieve the rest of your career goals."

Step 4: The Senselessness of Racism

During this part of the treatment, you will discuss with the client if they are trying to make sense of their experiences of racism and "figure it out." You must let the client know that racism does not make logical sense. Instead, it can be more helpful to provide a broader understanding of racialization and its impact on people's emotions, thoughts, and behavior. To do so, you will want to discuss the nature of racism and provide some background on its historical roots—beginning with colonialism, Whiteness, imperialism, capitalism, and the patriarchy—and frame them as toxic and destructive ideologies.

In addition, discuss how racism is systemic and embedded in social structures and institutions (e.g., in policies and procedures of hospitals, legal systems, and school systems). That means people who commit overt acts of racism are not just "bad apples"—the systemic nature of racism enables the behavior of individual racists. Racism is also maintained through cultural conditioning, wherein people of color are taught to defer, and White people are taught to be silent when racism happens. Here is how you might begin to introduce this conversation:

> *"Let's talk about the historical roots of racism for a moment. Racism and White supremacy have been around since the inception of this country and informed the development of our institutions—medical, legal, educational, and so on. The majority of people in power who developed and enforce our laws, policies, and standards of practice are White. Although some laws, policies, and practices have been changed in an attempt to right the wrongs of racism, people in power who still hold racist beliefs have found loopholes to maintain White supremacy and justify the mistreatment of people of color.*
>
> *"For example, although chattel slavery has been abolished, modern-day slavery continues in the form of forced labor as punishment for being convicted of a crime. Although people of color are no more likely to commit crimes, they are overrepresented in our prison system due to the over-policing of communities of color. Having a legal record then creates barriers to accessing social supports like food and housing when re-entering society and makes it difficult for people to get education or a job to support themselves.*
>
> *"We have been trained since birth to maintain these inequities that uphold structural racism. Specifically, White people are taught not to see racism and people of color are taught not to discuss it. People who act outside of these expectations are ostracized, causing social pressure to conform to these unspoken rules."*

Step 5: Describe the Connection Between Racism and PTSD (and Other Psychopathologies)

Racism is traumatizing! To connect the client's experiences of racism with their trauma symptoms, you'll want to review these common symptoms of PTSD with your client and ask whether they are experiencing any:

- Trying hard not to think about traumatic events from the past or recurring in the future
- Avoiding certain places, things, situations, or people because of their experiences (*Note*: This is a very common symptom that may make clients want to avoid coming to sessions.)
- Feeling ongoing fear, horror, anger, guilt, or shame
- Viewing themselves in a more negative way (e.g., "I should be stronger")
- Feeling like the world is a dangerous place
- Difficulty experiencing positive feelings or feeling emotionally numb
- Being overly alert or on guard (hypervigilance)
- Being jumpy or easily startled

- Night terrors
- Flashbacks (uncommon)

When reviewing these symptoms with the client, you can refer back to the assessment you conducted earlier. For example:

> *"There are many symptoms of racial trauma. I asked you about some of these during our assessment, but I want to review all the possible symptoms for you to make sure you have a full picture of what racism can do to people and to find out which of these symptoms are bothering you the most. I also want to answer any questions you might have about any of these."*

Psychoeducation Can Come in Many Forms

To bring the point to life, it can also be helpful to tell a story about the connection between racism and PTSD symptoms. This can be a story from the news, about someone you knew, or even about yourself.

> *"Allen was a young African American man working at a retail store. Although he enjoyed and valued his job, he struggled with the way he was treated by his employer.*
>
> *He was frequently demeaned, given menial tasks, and even required to track African American customers in the store to make sure they weren't stealing. He began to suffer from symptoms of depression, generalized anxiety, low self-esteem, and feelings of humiliation.*
>
> *After filing a complaint, he was threatened by his boss and then fired. Allen's symptoms worsened. He had intrusive thoughts, flashbacks, difficulty concentrating, irritability, and jumpiness—all symptoms of PTSD. Allen was found to be suffering from racial trauma.*
>
> *Allen later sued his employer for job-related discrimination, and five employees supported his allegations (Carter & Forsyth, 2009)."*

Step 6: Assign Homework Exercises

As part of therapy, your client will be completing weekly homework assignments that are intended to help them better understand racism and its impact. Explain that at this stage of the therapeutic process, the focus of these assignments will also be on developing personal strengths, and that they will eventually transition to processing experiences of racism. When discussing homework, make sure to reiterate the benefits of completing this between-session work:

> *"You and I will meet regularly to work through traumatic experiences of racism, but the majority of the work will happen outside of session in your everyday life. My hope is that you can apply what we discuss in session to what you experience outside of session. Our meetings together will give us an opportunity to discuss progress toward this goal. So, completing the between-session work will help you be successful in applying what we discuss to your everyday life."*

Over the course of the next week and beyond, ask the client to complete an empowerment journal, in which they will respond to weekly prompts and record any experiences of microaggressions or other forms of racism, as well as their thoughts and feelings pertaining to these microaggressions. For this week, the client should journal about their reactions to the physical toll of racism and any thoughts they have about the racism they experienced in light of the psychoeducation provided. The journal will be an important starting place in the next therapy session.

Invite the client to reach out by email during the week if they are having any difficulty with the exercise. Instruct them to read the following article before the next session as well.

Client reading in advance of the next session: Williams, M. T. (2015, September 6). The link between racism and PTSD. *Psychology Today*. https://www.psychologytoday.com/intl/blog/culturally-speaking/201509/the-link-between-racism-and-ptsd

Empowerment Journal: Reactions to the Physical Toll of Racism

This exercise you will allow you to delve into your personal experiences with the physical toll of racism. It offers you a safe space to reflect on your physical and emotional responses. By exploring these reactions, we can gain deeper insights into the impact of racism on your well-being and work to foster resilience and healing. Take some time to write your responses to the following questions:

1. Think of a recent experience where you believe racism had an impact on you physically. Describe this experience in detail.

   ____

   ____

   ____

2. List any physical reactions you experienced during or after the incident. These can include but are not limited to increased heart rate, muscle tension, or sweating.

   ____

   ____

   ____

3. Consider how these physical reactions to racism may impact your daily life and overall well-being. For example, are there situations or activities you avoid because of these reactions?

   ____

   ____

   ____

4. Take a moment to reflect on what you've written. Consider any patterns or recurring physical reactions you've noticed in response to racism. Think about how understanding these reactions can be a valuable step in addressing the impact of racism on your well-being.

   ____

   ____

   ____

Session 2: Coping and Self-Care

The main purpose of this session is to help the client make use of functional coping strategies against racism and to increase their level of self-care. The topic of self-compassion is also included here, as many clients do not feel they deserve self-care, and learning to have self-compassion can help them move forward. Nonetheless, you should continue to provide caring affirmations and look for opportunities to actively counter racial stereotypes.

Step 1: Review Homework

Every week, you will ask the client about their homework. It is important not to omit this step, or clients will think the homework is not important. For this session, this is your opportunity to review with the client the link between racism and PTSD, as highlighted in the reading, and ask the client if they have any questions about it.

Next, ask how things went with the empowerment journal. Invite the client to read or summarize some of what they wrote. They should have completed at least one entry, but ideally, they will have made three to four entries during the week. Make sure to give lots of supportive and positive feedback for any homework completed. If the homework was not done, review the importance of homework completion and troubleshoot around any problems they may have encountered. Then proceed by asking about any thoughts they had during the week with respect to what was covered in the last session.

Step 2: Assess Coping Strategies

Sometimes racialized people develop unhealthy strategies for coping with racism. You should assess whether clients are self-harming to cope, which may include misuse of substances, parasuicidal self-harm, suicidal ideation, dysfunctional eating, or other risk-taking behaviors. While you want to discourage these behaviors, it is important to remember that they serve a purpose (e.g., providing short-term, temporary relief). In addition, more beneficial approaches may not be available or readily apparent to the client.

Further, how you define the functionality of these coping strategies depends on whether the client's goal is to stop the distress caused by racist acts or to stop racism from occurring. Although strategies that relieve acute distress may have a more immediate impact on the client's emotional state, problem-focused strategies that seek to end ongoing racism (rather than simply helping the client endure it), represent a more useful means of coping and will help reduce racism in the person's life overall. While problem-focused strategies may increase distress in the short term, they result in greater well-being in the long term.

What's more is that some coping strategies are ambiguous in terms of whether they are helpful, as approaches that are useful for some clients may only increase stress and reduce functioning for others. This is why it is important to take an inventory of your client's coping strategies and evaluate their effectiveness in collaboration with the client. You should not label coping strategies in terms of whether they are "good" or "bad" but, rather, examine whether they are adaptive in their specific context, in both the short and long term—"helpful" versus "unhelpful." Some strategies will be deemed unhelpful, in which case you can help identify replacement strategies for the client. For ambiguous strategies (e.g., those that may be helpful in some contexts and unhelpful in others), you will need to conduct an ongoing assessment of the effect of said strategy before, during, and after the client responds to racism, and then make a determination as to whether or not adjustments are needed.

One strategy that is often overlooked but should be assessed is termed "John Henryism." This is a harmful coping mechanism that is often used by people of color, famously named after the fable of a Black man who died from exhaustion competing against a steam engine. This coping style is particularly prevalent among those who believe that enough hard work will eventually lead to them be successful and be recognized as equal to their White counterparts. This strategy can have positive results in the short term, as it can promote hard work and avoid conflict. However, in the long term, it can cause or accelerate debilitating physical ailments.

When asking the client to describe how they cope with racism in their life, make sure that they provide tangible examples (e.g., crying, punching a wall, calling a friend, eating chocolate). You might open the conversation by saying:

> *"If you're okay with it, I'd like to talk about how you respond when someone acts racist toward you or when you feel the impact of being a person of color in a racialized society. What do you do when these terrible experiences happen to you?"*

Referencing the client's assessment results on the Coping with Discrimination Scale (CDS) can be a good entry point into this discussion as well. You can point out how coping strategies differ in terms of how adaptive or maladaptive they are. Over the course of treatment, make sure to encourage the use of coping strategies that you and the client collaboratively determine are adaptive or healthy (several of which are described in the next sections). Reassure your client that change is a process and that you will work together as a team to help ensure that their coping responses are as healthy and effective as possible.

Step 3: Self-Compassion

Self-compassion involves treating yourself with kindness and understanding in the face of inadequacy, failure, or suffering. According to Kristin Neff (2003), self-compassion has three dimensions:

1. **Self-kindness versus self-judgment:** Being warm and loving toward oneself (rather than harsh or judgmental) during times of difficulty
2. **Mindfulness versus over-identification:** Acknowledging difficult feelings without getting caught up in them
3. **Common humanity versus isolation:** Recognizing that suffering and difficulties are part of a shared human experience rather than simply an isolated personal failure

Increasing self-compassion can decrease the guilt and shame that individuals might feel following experiences of racism. With self-compassion, they are reminded to extend feelings of love and kindness toward themselves while recognizing that others suffer in the same way as well. You can help a client with race-based trauma learn to cultivate self-compassion by encouraging them to nonjudgmentally focus on their immediate needs in the present. For example, you might say:

> *"I understand that you are frustrated with yourself for having to take a leave from work due to racial stress, but can you give yourself permission to feel unwell for a while? Everyone has times when they can't do all the things they would like due to illness, stress, or unexpected life events. How would it be to accept that you need a break—and that for now, that is okay?"*

Self-Compassion

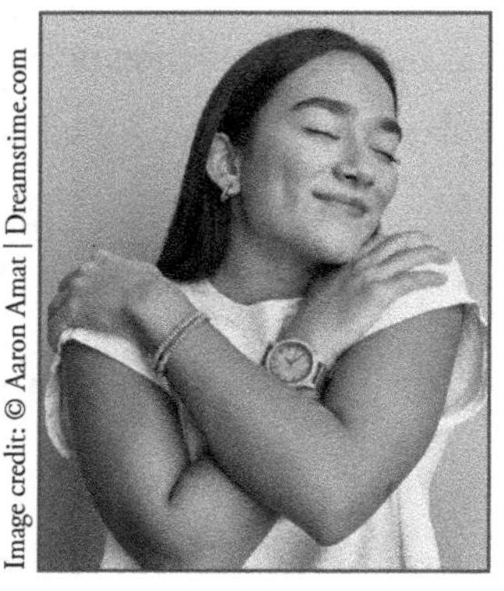

Image credit: © Aaron Amat | Dreamstime.com

Self-compassion helps clients develop resilience, reduces stress, and shifts the focus so they can recognize emotions but not act through them. It may be especially needed when clients are bombarded by racist messages or struggle with internalized racism.

Compassion-focused therapy goals:

- Love yourself
- Love others
- Accept love from others

Part of being able to cultivate a self-compassionate stance is the use of mindfulness, which grounds the client in the right here, right now. The use of mindfulness as a therapeutic approach was inspired by Buddhist traditions, but all religions have some form of contemplative practice, so it can be appropriate for people of all faiths or for those with no spiritual beliefs at all. Nonetheless, caution must be used when introducing mindfulness exercises, such as meditation, as they may be misconstrued as a competing religious practice, making clients uncomfortable to engage in such activities. You want to first gain an understanding of your client's beliefs so that mindfulness exercises can be made congruent with their existing religious practices and worldview.

With mindfulness, your client can learn how to pay attention to the present moment by nonjudgmentally noting their surroundings, physical sensations, and thoughts without becoming involved in them. This allows the client to become aware of their thoughts and feelings without getting caught up in ruminating about their personal struggles. You can use mindfulness in sessions by directing the client to focus on their body. For example, after they share an upsetting experience, you can say, "What are you feeling in your body right now as we talk about the security guard threatening you in that way?"

Individuals who practice mindfulness are less likely to participate in avoidance behaviors and are more likely to engage in actions that help them live a more meaningful, improved, and valued life. This is especially important for individuals who are experiencing racism, who may attempt to emotionally avoid or distract themselves from experiences of racism, leading to greater stress and depression. In fact, many people struggling with racial trauma have difficulty acknowledging their feelings about these experiences. Mindfulness can be a positive strategy for accepting the negative emotions caused by racist events.

However, mindfulness can be potentially unhelpful if it leads clients to accept repetitive mistreatment that, in turn, facilitates continued victimization due to racism. For example, a client of color might spend an hour meditating each day to lower their blood pressure due to stress from work, yet fail to consider looking for a different job. Therefore, you must take care to make sure that your client is practicing mindfulness in a way that facilitates their well-being.

There are many useful ways in which you can encourage your client to practice mindfulness, including through a loving-kindness guided meditation. There are guided meditations available that include affirmations specific for those seeking healing from racial trauma. You can select one of these meditations to play in session and offer it as an additional resource for clients to make use of outside of the therapy room.

Black Lives Matter Guided Meditation

Dr. Candace Nicole developed a Black Lives Matter guided meditation that includes mindfulness, affirmation, and loving-kindness. She created two versions: (1) a *Black Lives Matter Meditation for Healing Racial Trauma*, which has been shown to be beneficial in reducing race-based stress reactions among Black people (Hargons et al., 2022), and (2) the *Ally + Accomplice Meditation* for cultivating an anti-racist mindset. Both meditations are just under 20 minutes long and include affirmations specific for those seeking healing from racial trauma or cultivating an anti-racist mindset. These meditations can be played in session or offered as an additional resource to clients outside of the therapy room as needed. You can find these at: https://www.drcandicenicole.com/post/2016-07-black-lives-matter-meditation.

Step 4: Self-Care

Self-care can be defined as any activity that promotes someone's overall health and general well-being. It is vital for recovery from all types of physical and emotional stressors. Since self-care is a broad term, here I am specifically referring to self-focused behaviors that enhance a person's well-being. This can include exercising, engaging in enjoyable personal pursuits, taking a personal day off from work, shopping for fun, getting a massage, going to individual psychotherapy, practicing aromatherapy, going sightseeing, listening to music, turning off one's phone, unplugging from stressful social media, or engaging in spiritual practices. For clients with chaotic lives and stressful jobs, setting aside time alone may be particularly important.

Part of self-care when it comes to healing from racial trauma is also making sure the client minimizes their exposure to racism as much as possible. To introduce this idea, you might say one of the following:

- *"You need to allow yourself time to recover. During this period, you may want to limit exposure to racism. This may mean avoiding going into places where you know or suspect people will mistreat you. This is an important step in prioritizing your wellness. You will not avoid these places or people forever, but for now, it may be helpful to allow your heart and mind to have some peace while you are recovering and healing."*
- *"You need space to heal where you are not constantly being bombarded with small or large acts of racism. What are the major sources of your racial trauma currently? How can you minimize your interactions with these sources in a healthy way?"*

Unfortunately, the concept of self-care has been overlooked among people of color due to racialized notions of who deserves self-care and who doesn't. In addition, people from more collectivistic cultures can struggle with the idea of doing pleasurable things that appear to be just for themselves, as this feels selfish to them. Indeed, most clients that my colleagues have seen with racial trauma are reluctant to engage in self-care. If this is the case with your client, remind them that when someone has been debilitated by racism, it makes it difficult to meet family obligations or be of service to others. Therefore, taking time to fulfill their own personal wants and needs is essential if they want to maintain good physical and mental health. To help bring about change, you can work with your client to develop a self-care plan and even schedule days in the calendar when specific self-care activities will occur:

> *"How are you making sure that you are doing activities you enjoy on a regular basis? What are some ways you can engage in self-care more? How can you ensure you have the time or are making time to do these things?"*

To overcome client reluctance, you can frame unapologetic self-care as an act of empowerment in the face of racist social attitudes, which may label self-care behaviors as wasteful or indulgent when enjoyed by people of color, who may not be considered deserving. It can also help to make a distinction between regular self-care, which views self-care as a set of behaviors, and *radical* self-care, which is a tool for social justice and survival for racialized communities that promotes self-determination, self-preservation, and self-restoration in an environment of ongoing stress and oppression (Wyatt & Ampadu, 2022). Radical self-care encompasses practices and choices that are fundamentally transformative and deeply rooted in promoting one's well-being on a holistic level. It involves actively challenging the societal norms and personal behaviors that contribute to one's stress and depletion, and it requires a deep commitment to prioritizing one's health and happiness.

This form of self-care involves setting boundaries, advocating for one's needs, and making sometimes difficult decisions to protect and nurture one's mental, emotional, and physical well-being. It may involve addressing systemic issues and personal life choices that have long-term impacts on health and happiness, such as seeking therapy for mental health concerns, engaging in social or political activism, or making significant lifestyle or career changes. Radical self-care is deeply personal and often interwoven with a broader understanding of social justice, as it recognizes how societal factors like racism, sexism, and other forms of discrimination can cause wear and tear that erodes well-being.

> **"Caring for myself is not self-indulgence, it is self-preservation, and that is an act of political warfare."**
>
> –Audre Lorde

In practical terms, clients can engage in self-care by recognizing situations or people who might mistreat them, avoiding those situations when possible, and preparing coping approaches in advance of these situations when they are unavoidable. But sometimes environmental stressors are so severe that a larger change is needed, which might require changing jobs, homes, or social groups. For clients with the means to do so, time away could be an excellent way to jump-start self-care. Spending time in nature can also contribute to the healing process.

Can a Vacation Be the Key to Sustained Wellness?

Image credit: © IakovKalinin; iStock

In many European countries, people experiencing workplace burnout routinely take a few weeks off to recuperate at a relaxing all-inclusive Alpine mineral hot spring, called a *kur*. This is considered an important employee health benefit and the right of every worker. German researchers have found that patients undergoing a traditional kur at four spa clinics experienced long-term positive effects, including less pain and greater well-being, that lasted at least one year after the kur (Leuchtgens et al., 1999; Maretzki, 1987). Think about how culturally meaningful travel could provide distance from problems, space for recharging, and new perspectives.

Step 4: Assign Homework Exercises

Over the course of the next week, instruct your client to develop a self-care plan and schedule days in their calendar when specific self-care activities will occur. You, together with the client, can use the following worksheet to help the planning process and track their progress.

Client reading in advance of the next session: Williams, M. T. (2022, January 9). Self-care for the chronic and demoralizing stress of racism. *Psychology Today*. https://www.psychologytoday.com/us/blog/culturally-speaking/202201/self-care-the-chronic-and-demoralizing-stress-racism

Self-Care Worksheet

Self-care is an essential component of your well-being. It involves taking intentional actions to nurture your physical, emotional, and mental health. This worksheet will guide you in developing a personalized self-care plan. Remember, self-care is about showing kindness to yourself and prioritizing your needs.

1. **Physical self-care.** Taking care of your body is vital for overall well-being. It's important to pamper yourself and allow yourself to relax. Put a check mark by any activities you can commit to incorporating into your daily routine:
   - ❒ Regular exercise (e.g., taking a walk around the block, dancing)
   - ❒ Pampering yourself with relaxation (e.g., lying on the couch, reading a book, watching a movie)
   - ❒ Disconnecting from your devices for quiet time
   - ❒ Practicing yoga or meditation
   - ❒ Other: ______________________________

2. **Dietary self-care.** Nourishing your body with the right foods can have a significant impact on your well-being. Select any dietary self-care practices you'd like to incorporate into your routine:
   - ❒ Making your favorite foods throughout the week
   - ❒ Enjoying cultural comfort foods
   - ❒ Maintaining a healthy, well-balanced diet
   - ❒ Incorporating organic fruits and vegetables into your diet
   - ❒ Other: ______________________________

3. **Social self-care.** Engaging in social activities with people you enjoy can provide emotional support and connection. Check off any social activities you'd like to do regularly:
   - ❒ Having coffee or dinner with a friend
   - ❒ Going to the movies with friends
   - ❒ Attending sporting events
   - ❒ Hosting a family game night
   - ❒ Other: ______________________________

4. **Reflection and insights.** Take a moment to reflect on the self-care activities you've chosen. Why did you select these specific activities? How do you anticipate they will contribute to your overall well-being and happiness?

____

____

____

____

____

____

____

5. **Creating your self-care plan.** Now that you've identified some self-care activities that resonate with you, create a self-care plan for the upcoming week. Allocate specific times for each activity and commit to them.

Self-Care Activity	Day/Time	Duration

Session 3: Cultivating a Support Network

Social support is necessary to weather the violence of racism and the treatment process, as well as to maintain wellness after treatment is over. This session is focused on helping clients identify existing social supports and finding ways to reduce stress and provide resources for when racial stress occurs.

Step 1: Review Homework

Review the client's self-care plan and schedule of activities. How did they do? Praise all self-care attempts and encourage the client to continue to prioritize this critical component of healing.

Step 2: Hard Truths About Individual Racism

At this point, you will introduce the importance of understanding the personal challenges posed by racism and what to expect from racists. When people interact with others, they generally expect reciprocity. In other words, if you are kind to someone, you expect them to be kind in return. You generally don't expect people to harm you without a clear reason to do so. If clients do not understand the motivations behind people's racist actions, they will continue to be unprepared and shocked when these events occur, especially if they have been kind to the perpetrator. They will spend a lot of time and energy trying to figure out what they did wrong that caused the negative interaction and trying to make themselves seem more desirable to the racist. They might invent things they did wrong in their head and apologize to the racist in an attempt to make peace. They do not understand that isolated acts of kindness toward racists will not make them kind in return. Here is how you might have this discussion:

> *"As we have been discussing, I'd like to emphasize that you are not the problem; the problem is racism. The problem is that we live in a racialized society and not that you have a flaw or deficiency, like not being strong enough. There are some hard truths about living in a racialized, racist society that we should discuss if that's okay with you. Bad things happen to good people all the time that they don't deserve. You don't deserve the racism you have been experiencing."*

To highlight some of the hard truths your client is experiencing, you will want to make statements that are specific to their situation. For example:

- *"You are putting a lot of energy into getting people to like you who will never like you."*
- *"Unfortunately, as a person of color, some people will hate you, no matter what."*
- *"Working harder is only making your coworkers more jealous."*
- *"Your boss has no intention of promoting you."*
- *"Even if you stay quiet, they will still see you."*
- *"Winning this lawsuit will not get you the respect you deserve."*

It is likely that clients will react to this news with dismay. It can be hard to accept that cross-racial interactions are not as straightforward as they should be, especially if these strategies have worked for the client in the past. For other clients, this discussion will make sense right away and provide a sense of validation and relief. No matter how your client responds to these hard truths, you want to encourage them to share their reactions. Here are some questions you might ask:

- *"What feelings come up for you as we are having this difficult conversation?"*
- *"What have you been taught about our country that makes it hard to digest this?"*
- *"I notice you are wringing your hands. How is the discomfort showing up in your body?"*
- *"How does knowing that you are not the problem change your perspective?"*

You should validate any emotional responses to the exercise. If the client seems disconnected from their feelings or aloof, they may need some time to process the information, and you can revisit it later.

Step 3: Identify Existing Social Supports

One of the most successful and healthy coping mechanisms to combat the stress of racism is social support. Care from others helps clients to start addressing racism in their environment, process painful experiences, and continue challenging racism in their daily lives to maintain their growth and healing. In anticipation of this, it will be important to take steps to start building your client's support network. This can include family members, friends, dating partners, coworkers, neighbors, or anyone else who offers love, care, and support to the client. Social support may be particularly important for people who are part of collectivistic cultural groups, but everyone needs such support.

Image credit: © Syda Productions | Dreamstime.com

It is also important to know that due to a long and enduring history of institutional and medical racism, and the resulting cultural mistrust this has caused among people of color, clients with racial trauma may be less likely to seek formal mental health care and may encounter disapproval from family members if they do seek such care. For example, consider a client who is a university student living with his parents, who describes feeling unsupported by his family in seeking treatment, in part due to their mistrust of Western mental health care. As a therapist, you could address the client's feelings in several different ways:

- **Validating the client's experiences, providing support and affirmation:**
    - *"I know it can be really hard to reach out for help when people you love and respect aren't on the same page. Tell me more about how your family thinks you should deal with this. Do you think it could help to have a family meeting to help them understand just how much you are suffering and how I think I can help?"*
    - *"I know that many communities of color have low trust with professionals, especially with professionals who are White. Does this have anything to do with your family situation?"*
- **Providing psychoeducation about racism and mental health:**
    - *"What does your family think about all the racism you experience? After everything you have gone through, how do they imagine you can just keep going?"* [Let the client reply.] *"And how do you feel about that? You know, no one wants to feel like they've been beaten by it, and it is very common for people to feel like they just need to endure. But given what we know about racism, that just doesn't work forever. It takes a physical and emotional toll. And in this country, racism has been around for over 300 years, and it's not going away anytime soon."*
- **Providing validation and identifying external social support:**
    - *"What has it been like when you've shared your experiences of racism with your parents? I wonder if they truly understand what you are going through. Are they a good source of support when something bad happens at school?"*
    - *"Sometimes parents shield their children from their own personal experiences with racism. Parents may find their own experiences with racism too difficult to share or even think about. Do you think your parents might have experienced racism too? Are there friends, siblings, or other family members who might feel comfortable talking about their experiences with you if your parents are not?"*

Overcoming Client Mistrust

Many clients of color are wary of trusting medical professionals, and for good reason, which may be an obstacle in developing a trusting relationship with you. To help work through this mistrust and build a secure therapeutic relationship, you can:

- Ask the client about racism they have encountered from other providers (e.g., doctors, nurses, therapists—especially White providers).
- Address the emotional impact of this racism on the client.
- Ask about experiences in which the client has felt invalidated or harmed by other clinicians.
- Discuss the impact of these breaches on the client's ability to disclose race-based stressors with others.
- Discuss the client's reactions to these experiences and how this has shaped their expectations in therapy currently.

When people share their experiences of racism with those who have had similar experiences, they may feel a sense of kinship and understanding. When a person of color is able to share their experiences with trusted others, it also provides them an opportunity to emotionally process their racialized experiences and reexamine any faulty thinking (e.g., self-blame, shame, internalized racism). Connecting clients with other people in their own ethnoracial group can provide social support in the sense that the individual's experiences with racism may be best validated by others who have experienced the same thing, rather than people who might not have a thorough understanding of these experiences.

Clients may also benefit from connecting with people of color across different ethnoracial groups. However, you should be aware that racism can occur between groups of color (e.g., an Indigenous person can be racist toward a Black person or vice versa). This form of racism is somewhat different from that enacted by White people because it does not occur on a widespread level and is more individualistic. Importantly, racism between people of color also advances White supremacy by dividing groups. This form of racism can be hurtful and traumatizing, even feeling like a cultural betrayal. Victims might have thoughts like "We are all in this together. Why are you doing this to me?"

This might be a good place to open the conversation on racial identity development and ask the client about racism they may have experienced from other people of color, if this has not already been covered. You can ask, "How have your experiences been with people of color who are different from your own ethnic group?"

Likewise, clients likely have several White friends who may or may not be helpful sources of support in the face of racism. Many people of color have White friends who may have let them down when they needed allies. You can address this in the following way:

> *"Today I'd like to talk a bit more about Whiteness, and specifically White people. Some White people want to help and are interested in becoming an ally and confronting their implicit biases.*

Others are racist and do not want to change. What are some experiences you have had with White people? How do you feel about White people?

"Generally, White people do not realize how much pain they cause people of color. This is not making an excuse for them but simply to say they are unaware most of the time. If you have White friends, sometimes they will fall short and not have your back because they are unable to break from White solidarity—which is often harder to do than they realize. If you consider them friends, you should anticipate needing to educate them from time to time and be vulnerable, disclosing to them how certain actions or non-actions make you feel. It is very painful for White people to confront their own racism. This is no excuse, however. How have White friends been racist to you? How have you responded?"

Cross-Racial Friendships

Cross-racial friendships are mutually supportive, congenial, and emotionally intimate relationships between two persons of different ethnic or racial groups. Such friendships increase multicultural skills by providing new perspectives on race, racism, power, and privilege.

Did you know? Black people in the US have about 8 times as many Black friends as White friends. But White Americans have an astonishing 45 times as many White friends as Black friends (Public Religion Research Institute, 2022).

The implication of these findings is that when we talk about race in our personal lives, we are by and large discussing it with people who look like us. This creates barriers to mutual understanding and connection.

Image credit: © Rawpixel; iStockw

Many clients of color have stories to share about when they experienced racism and their White friends or colleagues stood by silently, and maybe only offered a word of comfort after the perpetrator was gone. You can respond in the following way:

"I am very sorry to hear that people you trusted didn't stand up for you. Unfortunately, when people see acts of racism, they are often paralyzed and don't know what to do in the moment, even people with good intentions or those who might consider themselves activists. It doesn't mean they thought it was okay. That's no excuse, of course, and unfortunately their silence only makes the problem worse."

Therapist reading about failures in allyship: Reed, S. (2019, January 10). *The damage of White feminism: An anecdote*. Chacruna Institute. https://chacruna.net/the-damage-of-white-feminism-an-anecdote

Step 4: Explore Ways to Create More Social Support

Many people with racial trauma do not have enough people in their existing network to provide them with needed support, so you and the client should brainstorm how they can enlarge their network. For example, they might reach out to someone important with whom they have lost touch (e.g., an old friend) or a nurturing but distant family member. You can also help the client search for local meetups, anti-racism groups, healing circles, or equity, diversity and inclusion (EDI) committees at work or school.

The following exercise can help you put all these steps together and connect your client with members of their social network who can provide affirming support for experiences of racism. This exercise encourages the client to create an interpersonal inventory they can use for quick reference. You can start the exercise in session and have them add to it as homework.

Support Network Inventory

This exercise is designed to help you assess, expand, and strengthen your social support network in the context of dealing with experiences of racism. Take some time to respond to the following prompts:

1. **List your friends and family.** Write down the names of your friends and family members whom you might talk to about experiences of racism. Put a star (*) by those who have been particularly understanding and empathetic. Cross out (X) any who "don't get it" or are critical.

2. **Share a racist experience.** Select one anti-racist contact from the list you've made. Reach out to them and share a racist experience you've had. On the following lines, note their name, their response to what you share, and the support you receive.

3. **Expand your network.**
    a. **Friends and family who understand racism:** Think about other individuals in your life, such as friends and family members, who have a good understanding of racism and are not overly critical, but whom you do not speak to as often. List these individuals below, and consider reaching out to them to expand your network of support and empathy.

b. **Reconnect with someone important:** Plan to reach out to someone important with whom you have lost touch. This could be an old friend, a cousin, or anyone you feel a connection with. Write down their name and your plan for reconnection.

____

____

____

____

____

4. **Expand your network further.** Consider joining affinity groups, such as meetups, anti-racism groups in your community, or equity, diversity, and inclusion (EDI) committees at work or school. These groups can provide opportunities to connect with like-minded individuals who share your values. List some groups you may be interested in below.

____

____

____

____

____

Step 5: Assign Homework Exercises

Encourage your client to continue practicing self-care and to incorporate the self-care activities they identified in session into their regular routine. If they are not already engaging in regular exercise, ask them to engage in 30 minutes of moderate-intensity physical activity three times per week as well, given its healing benefits.

In addition, have the client complete the Support Network Inventory and bring it to the next session. Encourage them to connect with a supportive friend or family member at least twice over the course of the next week, and have them write about the experience in their empowerment journal. Finally, ask them to respond to the following prompt in their empowerment journal as well:

> *"Consider the words of Martin Luther King Jr.: 'In the end, we will remember not the words of our enemies, but the silence of our friends.' Who has let you down when you felt you needed support? Think about times when you needed a racial justice ally and felt let down or betrayed by someone you thought you could count on. This might be a person of the same or a different race. Pick one to two experiences that come to mind and write about each of them in your empowerment journal."*

Client reading in advance of the next session: DeLapp, R. C. T., & Williams, M. T. (2016, July 19). Proactively coping with racism. *Psychology Today*. https://www.psychologytoday.com/us/blog/culturally-speaking/201607/proactively-coping-racism

Part 2—Healing the Wounds of Racism

In the journey toward healing from the deep wounds of racial trauma, it becomes evident that addressing the internalized aspects of racism is a crucial step. This chapter focuses on the use of cognitive restructuring and exposure exercises to help clients heal from the trauma of racism.

In chapter 4, you will:

- Equip yourself to support the client in their healing journey from racial trauma.
- Help the client dismantle internalized racism and offer affirmations to aid in this process.
- Help your client understand colorism and build their ethnoracial identity.
- Guide the client through exposure and processing of experiences of racism.
- Discover effective strategies to combat racism in various scenarios.

Chapter Overview

This chapter delves deeper into the intricate process of recovery and healing. Through a series of five sessions, you will guide clients on a transformative journey to unravel the complex web of ingrained beliefs and biases that have been shaped by their encounters with racism. You will start session 4 by providing psychoeducation to shed light on the concept of internalized racism and its connection to racial myths. You will facilitate defusion from internalized racism through acceptance of difficult feelings, cognitive restructuring, and cultural affirmations. You will then move on to examine the impact of colorism and challenge myths about skin color in session 5. By challenging these misconceptions, clients can help build their self-perception and strengthen their ethnoracial identity.

Sessions 6 and 7 center around the recounting of traumatic racial experiences by guiding clients through several different types of exposure activities, including imaginal exposure, written expression, and creative outlets to process their feelings and reactions. As you progress into session 8, clients begin to learn the skills necessary to confront racism head-on.

Session 4: Dismantling Internalized Racism

People of color may suffer from internalized racism because they believe certain myths about their group. The goal of this session is to reduce shame and increase feelings of belongingness by challenging these racial myths through the use of cognitive defusion and cognitive restructuring. You will also demonstrate appreciation of the client's cultural strengths through micro- and macroaffirmations to aid in this process.

Step 1: Review Homework

Begin by asking the client about their efforts at physical exercise and other forms of self-care and the impact this has had on their well-being. Keep in mind that clients may be feeling a bit better as a result of self-care, but they may not yet be willing to attribute these improvements to self-care, or they may not yet notice any improvements in how they feel.

Explore their responses on the *Support Network Inventory*, asking about any insights they gained and any challenges they faced while completing it. As part of this discussion, see whether the client was able to get together with supportive friends or family members over the last week, and explore how these connections affected their emotional state.

Furthermore, encourage clients to share their thoughts on the Martin Luther King Jr. quote and their experiences of feeling let down or betrayed when seeking support for racial justice issues. Additionally, discuss the assigned reading and how it relates to their experiences and perspectives on coping with racism.

You want to create an atmosphere of trust and empathy where clients feel comfortable expressing their emotions and thoughts freely. This will allow them to better apply what they've learned to their daily lives and address any obstacles they may encounter. Lastly, remember to provide consistent feedback, validation, and support throughout the session to foster a positive therapeutic relationship.

Step 2: Psychoeducation for Internalized Racism

Society's pervasive racial biases and discriminatory practices can influence how individuals perceive themselves and their racial identity. Some people of color may develop *internalized racism*, which refers to the process by which individuals from marginalized racial or ethnic groups internalize negative beliefs, stereotypes, and biases about their own racial identity. This can lead to the development of negative thoughts and feelings toward themselves. It is crucial to help clients understand that these thoughts and feelings are not an accurate representation of who they are as individuals but, rather, a result of the systemic racism that exists in society. These thoughts and emotions are not inherent or natural. Instead, they are shaped by the social, cultural, and historical context of racism. Here is how you might introduce this conversation:

> *"I want to talk about something that might resonate with you, given your experiences. It's about how sometimes, without even realizing it, we can start to believe the negative things that people say or think about our race or ethnic group. These messages can be subtle but leave you feeling like there is something wrong with you. Have you ever caught yourself thinking or feeling things about*

yourself that seem to reflect those negative ideas? Realizing this can be a big deal. But it's not about blaming yourself for thinking this way. It's more about understanding that these ideas come from outside, and they don't have to define you."

Some Symptoms of Internalized Racism

- Low self-esteem
- Self-blame
- Cultural disconnection
- Negative self-image
- Internalized stereotypes
- Shame and guilt
- Preference for the dominant culture
- Constant feelings of inadequacy
- Internal conflicts
- Impaired mental health

Step 3: Understanding Racial Myths

As a therapist, it is essential that you recognize and tackle the impact of societal myths about race in session. These myths manifest in various ways, such as biased educational placements or hurtful racial stereotypes. One pervasive myth is the blatantly false suggestion that genetic or biological differences between races underlie inequality, as this myth often portrays those with darker skin as less intelligent or valuable. Here are some common myths that perpetuate racial inequality and sustain White supremacy:

- **Darker-skinned people are more violent with criminal tendencies.** This myth wrongly associates skin color with criminality, reinforcing harmful stereotypes and contributing to fear, racial profiling, and discrimination in the criminal justice system.
- **White people are naturally more financially successful and responsible.** Perpetuating the idea that financial success is inherent to a particular race overlooks the historical and systemic factors that contribute to economic disparities, fostering an inaccurate narrative and perpetuating the myth of meritocracy.
- **White people are more civilized and culturally advanced.** This myth is based on the false notion that certain racial groups are more civilized or culturally sophisticated than others, dismissing the contributions and rich cultural practices of diverse communities across the globe.
- **Black people are athletically superior but intellectually inferior.** This false stereotype suggests that certain races are only valuable for their physical abilities, reinforcing the harmful notion that Black children should focus on sports and not higher education.
- **Indigenous peoples are inherently primitive and resistant to modernization.** This myth overlooks the diverse histories and accomplishments of Indigenous communities, and it ignores the impact of colonialism and systemic oppression on their social and economic development.

In this step, you want to help your client recognize how these racial myths have affected them personally, emotionally, and psychologically. Begin by creating a safe and open space for your client to discuss their experiences and concerns related to race. Explore the concept of racial myths, focusing on the harmful idea that genetic or biological differences between races exist and that darker-skinned individuals are inherently less intelligent or valuable. Share relevant research to provide a factual basis for your discussion (e.g., Cerdeña et al., 2020; Donovan et al., 2019; Evans, 2018; Hogarth, 2019).

> *"Let's talk about something you might've heard about—the idea that people's race or skin color can determine how smart they are or can say something about their character. It's a difficult topic, but it's important to discuss. Being smart isn't about what race you are. It's about a whole bunch of things, like where you grow up, the kind of education you get, and the experiences you have. The main idea here is that race doesn't decide how intelligent someone is. Leading organizations in genetics and anthropology have stated clearly that racial categories are socially constructed and don't genetically determine much of anything. The group differences we see in society are due to racism, not inherent ability."*

Step 4: Examine Racism from Individuals Who Are Supposed to Be Supportive

When clients experience racism from individuals and social structures that are supposed to offer support—such as human resources personnel, mentors, or superiors—it can be particularly distressing and damaging. It's a betrayal that compounds the already harmful nature of discrimination. It's akin to being denied a safety net while navigating through a societal system laden with racial landmines. These encounters can evoke a range of painful emotions, such as disappointment, anger, helplessness, and a deep sense of injustice. Furthermore, such experiences can create an environment of distrust and fear, making it difficult for individuals to seek help, voice their concerns, or advocate for their rights in the future.

The emotional toll of such discriminatory experiences often extends into a person's self-esteem and self-worth, undermining their sense of professional and personal self-efficacy. The reality or anticipation of racial discrimination in supposedly supportive environments can also foster a chronic state of anxiety and hypervigilance, leading to a significant amount of psychological distress over time. Helping clients navigate and process these painful experiences is an essential first step toward healing and empowerment. Here, you can spend a little time reviewing and discussing these experiences. This not meant to be a deep dive, but a small detour to help clients gain more understanding surrounding their own anxieties and to ease them into the coming sessions where more focused attention will be on exposure and processing racist events.

The Illusion of a Safety Net

Racism pervades all areas of society, ranging from universities to the legal system. Many clients have been let down by systems that were supposed to protect them from racial abuse, such as superiors, human resources offices, ethics committees, and so on. Throughout treatment, you will help clients process these experiences by:

- Processing past breaches of trust and the ways in which the client felt invalidated and harmed by these systems.
- Discussing the impact of disclosing race-based stressors with administrators or other professionals: *"How did others react when you told them about your experiences of racism? What about other professionals or administrators, like the human resources office? How did they react when you shared this with them? What did they do?"*
- Discussing the client's reactions to these experiences and how this has led the client to therapy currently. The process of therapeutic responding might look as follows:
  - **Review:** Talk through the client's experiences with racism. Do not question the client's experiences; instead, be supportive and validating (which hopefully you have been doing all along!).
  - **Identify:** Discuss the faulty beliefs or cognitive distortions the client may be endorsing that are tied to their experiences of racism (e.g., self-blame).
  - **Perspective:** Propose a counternarrative (i.e., the opposite of what the client believes about themselves).
  - **Check in:** Ask the client how that sounds (logically) and how it feels (emotionally).

Step 5: Defusion from Internalized Racism

Internalized racism can cause immense shame and self-blame among racialized people. At the same time, given the insidiousness of racism, even people of color with a strong ethnoracial identity who do *not* experience self-hate or low self-esteem may internalize negative messages about their racial group. It can be especially hard for these clients when they realize the ways in which they experience internalized racism may unintentionally contribute to maintaining White dominance.

When individuals are suffering from internalized racism, your goal is to help them understand that their negative thoughts and feelings are a product of context (i.e., racism) and not an accurate description of the self. You want to help your client defuse from these ideas by (1) teaching them about the automatic nature of these negative thoughts, (2) helping them recognize that the presence of the thought does not mean it is true, but that it is a product of our racist environment, and (3) teaching the client to allow the thought to leave on its own without overinterpreting or acting on it in a counterproductive way.

Part of helping clients defuse from negative feelings about themselves will be dictated by how you, as the therapist, treat them. You want them to think positively about their race, ethnicity, and culture, and to be able to easily dismiss inaccurate thoughts that may intrude into their minds. To this end, you need to show that you are dismissive of racial falsehood and that you feel positively about the client's ethnoracial identity and culture. You will need to continually communicate your appreciation for your client as a product of their culture. Showing your own appreciation for their uniqueness as a member of their ethnoracial group will help build self-esteem and erode internalized racism. You can show your positivity through the use of both micro- and macroaffirmations.

Examples of Microaffirmations

Racial microaffirmations are small acts that help people of color feel supported. The following therapist statements reflect the use of microaffirmations to uplift and encourage the client while fostering an anti-stereotypical and inclusive environment.

- **Validation of cultural experiences:**

  "Your insight about your workplace experiences, and how these experiences interact with your cultural identity, is so important. It helps us understand and navigate these challenges together."

- **Acknowledgment of resilience:**

  "Your ability to persevere through the obstacles you've encountered at college demonstrates incredible patience and perseverance."

- **Empowerment through identity:**

  "Your unique blend of cultural identity and creativity in your work is a powerful testament to the Black experience. Embracing your heritage enriches the quality of the products you develop."

- **Encouragement of self-expression:**

  "Your thoughts and feelings about your journey as a first-generation immigrant are inspiring. Your voice matters, and it's important."

- **Support for cultural exploration:**

  "Exploring your cultural heritage and its significance while studying abroad can be an enriching experience. What excellent perspectives and observations you've made about America."

Examples of Macroaffirmations

Racial macroaffirmations are positive statements or other affirmations focused on embracing and celebrating one's racial or ethnic identity, and affirming the value and dignity of that identity in a broader societal context. Here are some macroaffirmations a therapist might say to a client, naming the client's specific ethnoracial group as appropriate.

- *"I admire the strength and resilience of your cultural community."*
- *"I'm standing with you in the fight against racial injustice."*
- *"I recognize the challenges you face because of your race, and I'm here to support you."*
- *"Your cultural heritage enriches our community and our world."*

To foster your ability to be an affirming source of cultural support, you can complete the following therapist exercise. If you have trouble completing this exercise and cannot think of anything your client has shared about their culture, find reasons to get curious and ask more about their heritage, family, and community during sessions. Ask them to share with you what gives them pride in their ethnic group. You can use questions from the *DSM-5* Cultural Formulation Interview (APA, 2013), which was introduced in chapter 2, to learn more about the role that cultural identity plays in their life. At the same time, if you find that you are unfamiliar with a client's ethnic group, make sure to do some work on your own to learn more about it so the client is not the sole source of education.

You can also help your client identify role models and other sources of support who are members of the same ethnoracial group. If a client has difficulty identifying social supports who share their identity, work together to brainstorm ways in which the client might develop these sources of support in their communities (e.g., reaching out to a relative or friend of the family they would like to become closer to).

Finally, you can use ethnic identity measures, such as the Multigroup Ethnic Identity Measure discussed in chapter 2, to assess the strength of a client's ethnic identity. Items on which the client scores low might be targets for strengthening. For example, if a client scores low on "I am active in organizations or social groups that include mostly members of my own ethnic group," the goal might be to brainstorm ideas for getting them involved in social groups of people from their ethnic identity (e.g., joining a Black church or Black fraternity/sorority).

Cultivating Cultural Awareness and Support for Clients of Color

To develop a deeper understanding of your client's cultural backgrounds and actively incorporate cultural sources of strength into therapy sessions, reflect on the following questions:

1. **Reflect on individual clients.** Take some time to think about each of your clients of color individually. Consider what they have shared with you about their culture, experiences, and challenges related to race and ethnicity. (You may wish to use additional paper for this and the next few prompts, especially if you see more than a few clients of color.)
   - Client 1: ______________________________
   ____
   ____
   - Client 2: ______________________________
   ____
   ____
   - Client 3: ______________________________
   ____
   ____
2. **Identify cultural sources of strength.** For each client, make a list of the cultural sources of strength that stand out to you. These may include cultural traditions, values, family dynamics, resilience, or any other aspects of their culture that contribute to their well-being.
   - Client 1: ______________________________
   ____
   ____
   - Client 2: ______________________________
   ____
   ____

- Client 3: ____

____

____

3. **Recognize cultural admiration.** Reflect on the facets of each client's culture that you genuinely admire. What aspects of their cultural background do you find particularly inspiring or valuable? Be specific in identifying these attributes.
    - Client 1: ____

      ____

      ____

    - Client 2: ____

      ____

      ____

    - Client 3: ____

      ____

      ____

4. **Integrate cultural strengths and customize your approach.** During your therapy sessions with each client, actively seek opportunities to share and validate the cultural strengths you've identified. This may involve acknowledging their resilience, appreciating their cultural practices, or discussing the importance of their ethnic identity. Remember that each client is unique, and their ethnic group significantly influences their experiences. Adapt your therapeutic approach to align with their individual needs and cultural preferences. In what unique way does each client need you to show up for them?
    - Client 1: ____

      ____

      ____

    - Client 2: ____

      ____

      ____

    - Client 3: ____

      ____

      ____

5. **Engage in continuous self-education.** Commit to ongoing self-education in the realm of cultural competence. Stay informed about issues related to race, ethnicity, and cultural diversity to enhance your ability to support your clients effectively. Do you notice any holes in your knowledge that should be filled? Below, identify your personal learning goals, the resources or training needed to achieve these goals, and your timeline for completing them.

6. **Reflection.**

   - How did this exercise help you gain a deeper appreciation for your clients' cultural backgrounds?

   - What strategies can you implement to ensure that cultural sources of strength are integrated into your therapy sessions effectively?

   - How can you create a more inclusive and culturally sensitive therapeutic environment for your clients of color?

Step 6: Assign Homework Exercises

At this point, your client will begin completing homework assignments that are intended to help them better identify racist experiences and their impact. Explain to the client that, for now, the focus of these assignments is about processing racist experiences and that they will eventually transition to identifying ways to respond to racism that will work better for them in the long run.

To start this process, encourage your client to complete the following log whenever they encounter a microaggression over the course of the next week and beyond. They can write about microaggressions they personally experience or those they witness. They will also log their automatic thoughts about themselves and the world as a result of the microaggression. This log will be a valuable tool for self-awareness and personal growth, and it will help you know how to best prepare cognitive and behavioral interventions to help the client combat racism, which will be discussed more in sessions 6 and 8. Notably, the negative thoughts the client has about themselves will likely be triggered by these experiences, which will help you determine how to focus your work around cognitive restructuring. You will also see whether the client's behaviors in response to racism are ineffective or counterproductive, allowing you to teach them better ways to respond when these events occur in the future.

Client readings in advance of the next session:

Sue, D. W. (2010, November 17). Microaggressions: More than just race. *Psychology Today*. https://www.psychologytoday.com/us/blog/microaggressions-in-everyday-life/201011/microaggressions-more-just-race

Kolbert, E. (2018, March 12). There is no scientific basis for race—it's a made-up label. *National Geographic*. www.nationalgeographic.com/magazine/2018/04/race-genetics-science-africa

Microaggressions Log

This worksheet is designed to help you track and reflect on instances of microaggressions you encounter. By doing so, you can better understand their impact, develop coping strategies, and explore more effective responses. You can make copies of this template to use whenever you experience a microaggression or reference these prompts while keeping a log in your journal.

1. **Description of the microaggression.** Describe the microaggression, including what was said or done.

    ____

    ____

    ____

    ____

2. **When did it happen?**

    Date: ______________ Time: ______________

3. **Where did it happen?**

    ____

4. **Why do you think it happened?** Reflect on the possible reasons behind the microaggression. What factors or biases might have contributed?

    ____

    ____

    ____

    ____

5. **Automatic self-talk generated.** Note any immediate thoughts or feelings that arose in response to the microaggression, about yourself and about the world in general.

    ____

    ____

    ____

    ____

6. **How you responded in the moment.** Describe what you said or did after the microaggression occurred.

____

____

____

____

7. **How you wish you would have responded in retrospect.** Describe what you wish you would have said or done instead.

____

____

____

____

8. **What got in the way.** Identify any barriers or challenges that prevented you from responding as you wished in the moment.

____

____

____

____

9. **Reflection.** Take a moment to reflect on the microaggression you've logged. Consider the impact it had on you, both emotionally and mentally. Reflect on possible strategies you can use to respond to similar situations in the future.

____

____

____

____

Session 5: Understanding Colorism and Building Ethnoracial Identity

Negative stereotypes about people of color may cause some clients to distance themselves from their ethnoracial group. To help clients combat these stereotypes, this session is focused on understanding and addressing colorism. This is supported by strengthening the client's ethnoracial identity via psychoeducation and by encouraging cultural engagement.

Step 1: Review Homework

Start by reviewing the client's *Microaggressions Log*. Encourage them to share any insights they noticed. For example, how did the exercise impact their awareness of racism in their environment? Did they notice any patterns in how they tend to respond to such incidents? Determine if the exercise has led to improved self-awareness and growth in terms of how the client views themselves in connection with racism. If the client did not do this exercise, troubleshoot around causes. Sometimes clients find it stressful to dwell on microaggressions, especially if their way of coping is by "not thinking about it." This log will be needed for future sessions, so it is important that they engage as much as possible.

Discuss the reading assignments, starting with Sue's (2010) article on microaggressions, and inquire about the key takeaways and connections the client made to their own experiences. Additionally, explore the *National Geographic* article by Kolbert (2018) on the concept of race and its implications. Encourage your client to share any reflections or emotions that arose in relation to the readings.

Step 2: Understanding Colorism

When people believe that different races have inherent genetic differences, they are more likely to accept and spread racist ideas and stereotypes. It can also lead to what's known as *skin-tone trauma* among individuals with darker skin, which is the traumatic stress that can occur when someone experiences colorism. Colorism is a type of prejudice that can occur within or between racial or ethnic groups, in which those with lighter skin shades are favored and those with darker skin are discriminated against. For example, one investigation found that darker-skinned Black Americans have lower socioeconomic status, are treated more harshly by the criminal justice system, enjoy diminished prestige, and are less likely to hold elective offices compared with their lighter-skinned counterparts (Hochschild & Weaver, 2007).

Colorism serves to promote Eurocentric standards of appearance and beauty. Here are some examples of colorism and the problems they can cause clients:

- **Treating darker-skinned people as if they are more dangerous.** This can lead to chronic stress, anxiety disorders, and heightened vigilance in people of color, and this is particularly salient for dark-skinned men. The constant stress of being perceived as a threat can lead to physical health issues as well, including hypertension and heart disease, due to the chronic activation of the stress response.

- **Using filters to lighten people's facial features on social media.** This practice can make people of color feel unattractive and exacerbate body dysmorphia, depression, and anxiety about one's appearance. The persistent dissatisfaction with one's physical appearance can also lead to unhealthy behaviors to compensate, such as eating disorders.
- **Casting in the film industry with a preference for lighter-skinned Black women over darker-skinned ones.** Celebrities are often role models for the public, especially youth, and this kind of exclusion can contribute to feelings of low self-worth and identity struggles in darker-skinned women, potentially leading to depression and anxiety.
- **Using commercial products for skin lightening, which are especially popular in countries like India.** The pressure to use such products can result in permanent skin damage and other health issues due to the harmful chemicals often found in them. Psychologically, it can lead to issues like depression and social anxiety stemming from a deep-seated dissatisfaction with one's appearance.
- **Elevating blonde-haired women as the standard of female beauty.** This sidelines individuals with darker features, reinforcing a narrow definition of attractiveness. This can lead to a range of mental health issues, including depression, anxiety, and low self-esteem among those who feel they don't meet these beauty standards.
- **Treating lighter-skinned children in a family better than darker-skinned ones.** This can result in long-term psychological trauma, low self-esteem, and issues with familial attachment and trust. It can lead to depression, anxiety, and an increased risk of developing a range of mental health disorders.
- **Calling straighter hair "good hair" and curlier hair "bad hair."** The pressure to alter one's natural hair can contribute to negative self-image and low self-worth. It can result in physical damage to the hair and scalp due to the use of harsh chemicals and flat irons, as well as the psychological stress associated with maintaining a modified appearance.

Colorism Experienced by a Japanese American Woman Growing Up

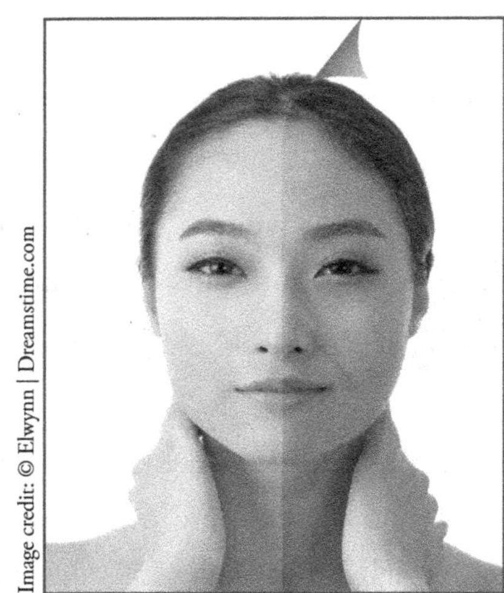
Image credit: © Elwynn | Dreamstime.com

In her essay *Too Dark* (2020), Miho Iwata shares her experience with colorism: "My dark skin was challenged by different sets of audiences. Due to the cultural preference for white skin, many Asian and Asian American friends frequently shared their alarm about my dark complexion. I remember some of them asking me why I liked to go to the beach and 'risk' getting tanned, or why I did not wear sunscreen. This negativity would follow me across the Pacific when I visited my family and friends in Japan. There, my very tanned skin was seen as 'deviant,' particularly given my age. When I was a little girl, my dark complexion was somewhat acceptable. However, having dark skin as a woman in Japan is seen as very problematic. . . . Over the years, I have noticed how people around me interpret and react to my changing complexion, and their appraisals are largely influenced by my gender, place, and age." (pp. 50–51)

Repeated exposure to colorism can lead a client to develop a negative self-image, where they may come to view their skin color as a personal flaw. If their skin color is perceived by others as different from stereotypical people in their ethnoracial group (e.g., an African American with light skin), it can also lead to an identity conflict, which can negatively impact a person's self-esteem. To better understand your client's experiences with colorism, discuss the concept of skin-tone trauma and guide them in identifying instances where they may have encountered colorism their life. You can also use the following exercise to help them reflect on messages they have received throughout their lifetime about skin tones.

Reflecting on Childhood Messages About Skin Color

Internalized beliefs about skin color can be subtle and deeply ingrained. For this exercise, take some time to reflect on messages you may have learned about your own skin color during your childhood.

1. **Identify the messages you learned.** What messages or beliefs about your skin color did you absorb while growing up? These messages might have come from family, friends, school, the media, or society in general. Jot down at least three specific messages or beliefs.
   - Message 1: ______________________________
   - Message 2: ______________________________
   - Message 3: ______________________________
2. **Reflect on the impact of these messages.** Consider how these messages influenced your feelings about yourself throughout childhood and adolescence. Did they impact your self-esteem, self-worth, or self-confidence? How did you react to these messages emotionally and psychologically?
   - Impact of message 1: ______________________________
   - Impact of message 2: ______________________________
   - Impact of message 3: ______________________________

3. **Connect to your present.** Reflect on whether any of these childhood messages still affect your self-perception today. Do you find that you've carried any of these beliefs into your adult life, even unconsciously? Consider if they impact your decision-making, relationships, or thoughts about yourself.

____

____

____

____

____

4. **Strategies for change.** Think about steps you can take to challenge and redefine these messages about your skin color. How would you like to feel about yourself and your skin color moving forward? List at least three strategies or actions you can implement to build a more positive and empowering relationship with your skin color. Here are some strategies you might consider:

   - **Self-affirmations:** Repeat positive affirmations to yourself each day that celebrate the unique beauty of your skin color. Look in the mirror and love your skin. Remind yourself of your inherent worth and recognize any lingering negative beliefs from childhood.
   - **Diversify your media consumption:** Surround yourself with diverse representations of beauty in media. Seek out content that embraces various skin tones and challenges conventional standards, promoting a more inclusive and affirming perspective.
   - **Social support:** Connect with others who have had similar experiences or have successfully navigated the journey of challenging these toxic societal norms to deepen your understanding and resilience.
   - Strategy 1: _______________

     ____

     ____
   - Strategy 2: _______________

     ____

     ____
   - Strategy 3: _______________

     ____

     ____

Step 3: Challenging Myths About Skin Color

Debunking racial myths is a vital part of the therapeutic work. You must guide your client in confronting and dispelling these myths so they can understand that societal disparities aren't rooted in innate factors tied to skin color. This will help further reduce the shame that they may be experiencing and increase their feelings of belongingness. It also helps promote a more inclusive and equitable society.

When debunking racial myths, the quality of your psychoeducation will be key. Many people are used to thinking about race as they would breeds of dogs—as something tangible, familiar, and scientific—when it is, in reality, unscientific and supremist. Part of the confusion around genes and race stems from our understanding of how genes define heritable traits (such as height, blood type, and skin color) and then mashing this together with assumptions about how related individuals may be based on skin hue. Unfortunately, this is as sensible as assuming, for example, that individuals must be biologically related because they are the same height or that skunks and pandas may be highly related because both have black-and-white fur.

It can be important to explain to the client how the concept of "race" is inconsistent with population genetics and that humans cannot be categorized neatly into biologically distinct subcategories. The ongoing mixture between populations further erodes genetic distinctions. Some clients may have a hard time believing that race is not a biological category, as it is so firmly embedded in individuals at all educational levels—up to and including university professors. However, common sense can be helpful in this discussion, as it may be easier to explain that it does not make sense that a White mother and her Black child could be highly related (sharing 50 percent of their genes) but be called different "races" based on skin hue. In addition, people categorized as "Black" in America have, on average, 25 percent European ancestry but can have up to 90 percent European ancestry (Bryc et al., 2015).

Ultimately, the concept of race as a biological category is a myth that was implemented in colonial America so that White slaveowners could legally and barbarically own and sell their darker-skinned children. Known as the "one-drop rule," it allowed any individual with even a single drop of "Black blood" to be categorized as Black. Using concrete examples such as this can help illustrate the real-world impact of these myths. You can also discuss recent examples of biased educational placements and differences in health outcomes between racial groups that are due to racism rather than genes:

> *"To help you better grasp this concept, let's consider some real-life examples. In the United States, we've seen that African and Caribbean children with darker skin tones often excel academically. This challenges the idea that race determines intelligence or ability. Additionally, when we look at the effects of environmental pollution and lead poisoning, which seriously affect children's cognitive functioning and brain development, we find that these practices disproportionately harm Black communities. This is another clear example that shows how external factors, and not genes, can impact success and well-being."*

Image credit: © Prostock-Studio; iStock

Your goal is to present alternative perspectives and narratives that promote equality and inclusivity. This will be accomplished, in part, by sharing research-based facts demonstrating that societal disparities are not due to innate factors linked to skin color.

For example, consider a client who shares with you that she feels unattractive due to her skin color. This can be a result of problems like colorism, leading to low self-esteem. You can use a number of approaches to address this, based on what you believe would best resonate for the client. For example, it can help to know that even glamorous people have struggled with these issues and have also overcome them. In this case, you could use storytelling to bring about a change in perspective and say:

> *"In 2014,* People *magazine named Lupita Nyong'o the Most Beautiful Woman in the World. At a major Hollywood event, she gave a powerful speech where she described feeling very "un-beautiful" as a child, when she would pray for lighter skin. As a Kenyan-Mexican actress, Lupita is only the third Black woman to be named* People's *Most Beautiful Woman since the magazine started giving out the title in 1990. Prior to that, Halle Berry and Beyoncé were the only African Americans who were recognized. And as beautiful as they are, they have very light skin, which makes them closer to Hollywood's Eurocentric standard. Lupita was thrilled to be on the cover of* People *magazine because of "all the girls who would see me on it and feel a little more seen," she said. She shared that when she was younger, she thought beauty was what you saw in the media, stating, "Light skin and long, flowing, straight hair . . . Subconsciously you start to appreciate those things more than what you possess (Yahr, 2014)."*

You could also provide psychoeducation about the merits of dark skin:

> *"Your skin is brown because it is rich in melanin. It will be soft and smooth 20 years from now and still look amazing when your friends without melanin have wrinkles and are getting Botox. Melanin even helps to protect you from UV rays, lowering your risk of skin cancer. That is truly a gift. Don't let anyone tell you otherwise."*

Alternately, you could take an FAP-based interpersonal approach and be a corrective mirror:

> [Showing a look of surprise and sadness on your face] *"I feel a pain in my heart when you say that. Do you want to know what I see when I look at your skin?"* [Let the client reply.] *"Your skin is beautiful!"*

Step 4: Strengthening Ethnoracial Identity

As discussed in chapter 1, ethnic identity development is a multifaceted construct that describes how people develop a sense of belonging to their culture. Building a strong, positive ethnoracial identity is essential for the mental health and well-being of people of color, including biracial and multiracial people as well as immigrants of color. It is also a key foundation for building self-identity because it provides people with a sense of identification with group cultural values, kinship, and beliefs. Therefore, strengthening a client's ethnoracial identity is an important way to help combat negative cognitions they may have about their group or their self-worth.

Clients who did not receive enough positive messages about their ethnoracial group growing up may need to be re-educated and supported in appreciating and developing a healthy ethnoracial identity. You can do so by:

- Helping the client gain an appreciation of their group by acquiring more cultural and historical knowledge
- Enhancing the client's connectedness to their group by practicing cultural traditions
- Teaching and celebrating cultural strengths to mitigate the impact of ethnoracial trauma
- Encouraging critical thinking about presumed racial differences to dispel myths about race
- Promoting a healthy sense of cultural skepticism, such as questioning White supremacy and the individuals and systems that support it
- Teaching the client about the nature of racism
- Supporting the client in figuring out what their ethnic group and race mean to them personally

Clients can also strengthen their identity through the experience of *racial uplifts*, which are defined as culturally positive experiences that can occur in everyday moments. Some racially uplifting experiences may include having conversations about overcoming racial obstacles, engaging in activities that demonstrate competence in two or more cultures, seeing members of their racial group depicted in a positive light, or enjoying music from an artist of the same ethnoracial group. (As a note, this definition is not the same as the concept of racial uplifts that emphasizes how members of racialized groups can improve their social and economic standing through individual effort and collective action.)

It is common for therapists to be so concerned about offending clients that they say nothing about the client's race, ethnicity, or culture, even when the client brings it up. However, this silence only reinforces the notion that there is something shameful about the client's identity—so shameful, in fact, that it cannot be discussed. You can directly support a client's ethnoracial growth by engaging in deliberate supportive statements, such as racial uplifts or micro- and macroaffirmations, as discussed previously.

Get Creative! Building Cultural Pride Through Nail Art

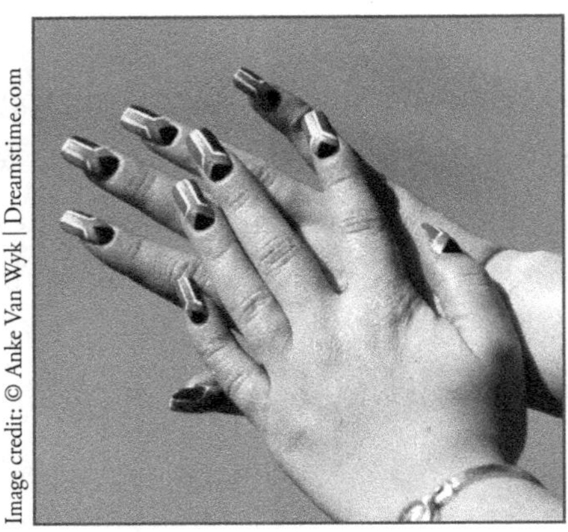
Image credit: © Anke Van Wyk | Dreamstime.com

Nail art that draws inspiration from national flags or symbols can serve as a creative expression of self-care and cultural pride. The careful process of manicuring and painting nails is a therapeutic act, offering a moment of relaxation and personal attention that can uplift one's mood and boost self-esteem. Simultaneously, by incorporating the vivid colors and symbols of a country's flag, people can carry a piece of their heritage with them, providing a daily reminder of their roots and community. This form of artistic expression also acts as a conversation starter, allowing people to connect with others over a shared culture or to share aspects of their culture with people from different backgrounds. Ultimately, this blend of self-care and cultural celebration can help move clients toward a sense of belonging and pride, enhancing personal well-being and ethnic identity.

Step 5: Cognitive Restructuring

Cognitive restructuring is a core component of many first-line treatments for PTSD, where therapists collaborate with clients to identify stuck points, evaluate the existing evidence for these stuck points, and generate more balanced and adaptive beliefs. As described in session 1, clients who have experienced racial trauma often hold several common cognitive distortions, including the thought that they are:

- Not worthy
- Not smart
- Not strong enough or weak
- Invisible
- Unlovable
- Unattractive
- Incapable of achieving their goals

Image credit: © Wavebreakmedia; iStock

To assist your client in restructuring any cognitive distortions they may hold as a result of internalized racism, you will want to help them make sense of their experiences by placing them in their appropriate sociohistorical context. Take care not to reinforce any faulty beliefs that the client has about the perceived low value of their ethnoracial group. You should also not remain silent in the face of a client's shame or self-blame. Rather, you should identify any comments the client makes that degrade their racial or ethnic group and discuss these in a non-shaming manner together with the client. For example, consider the client pictured here, who shares a dream about feeling invisible. Can you identify the internalized racism in the theme of the dream? There are several techniques we have reviewed that can be used to address this. You might say:

> *"Your dream seems to touch on feelings about your racial identity and societal perceptions about being a Black woman. You are not imagining it; it is real. But what concerns me is that it sounds like you might be internalizing some of the messages our racist society has been sending you. These are systemic issues that aren't a reflection of your worth or capabilities at all. Let's talk about how we can nurture your sense of identity and belonging in the face of these challenges. What can we do to make sure your voice is better heard?"*

The fundamental objective of CBT with clients who suffer from internalized racism is to help them become more aware of, confront, and alter their negative thoughts and beliefs about themselves and their ethnic group. Modifying dysfunctional core beliefs can begin once clients have learned how to recognize negative automatic thoughts and their accompanying emotional, behavioral, or physiological consequences.

You can help clients externalize the impact of racial stressors by exploring factors outside themselves that better explain discrimination-related events, such as the perpetrator's own prejudice and biases, and thereby minimize internalization of negative race-based messages. Take, for example, a Black college student who has developed core beliefs reflecting White supremacist ideology and who blames herself for not being smart or capable because she keeps failing school tests. To deal with the client's internalized racism, you must externalize the oppression by questioning the client's beliefs and critically challenging them to bring about a change in thinking. You want to help her see that the problem is separate from herself. The first step in this process would be to increase the client's awareness of any negative automatic thoughts that reflect internalized racism. For example, she may think that she is not smart enough to finish school because she holds the belief that Black people are not as smart as White people.

CLIENT: *I keep failing my math tests, and it feels like I'm just not smart enough. It's like everyone just expects me to fail because I'm Black, and there's this belief that we're not as intelligent. For me, it feels like it's true.*

THERAPIST: *I hear how challenging this has been for you. It sounds like there might be an added layer related to race in your experience. I think it can be hard to focus when all you can think about is validating a stereotype.*

CLIENT: *Exactly! I feel like I'm under a microscope and it's so distracting. I read things over and over and I'm so worked up I just can't take it in.*

THERAPIST: *So, it sounds to me like your struggles are not a reflection of your intelligence but all these racial stressors. I have a hunch you would do so much better in this class if you weren't so worried.*

CLIENT: *Oh, definitely.*

THERAPIST: *So, your performance doesn't have anything to do with your inherent "smarts"—it's all this anxiety. Let's talk about how we can change this negative thinking.*

Next, you would want to ask the client to keep a journal of her negative automatic thoughts to help her identify and challenge recurring patterns. After identifying any pattern, work with her to review whether the evidence supports those thoughts, or if there are alternate explanations (e.g., failing tests because of test anxiety or stereotype threat, rather than not being smart).

The final stage in this approach is to help the client discover new and more functional core race-related beliefs.

THERAPIST: *Let's consider some new and more useful beliefs about yourself. Maybe it's time to embrace all the amazing things your brain can do. For instance, instead of listening to that voice that says you're not smart enough, what if we explored affirming thoughts that highlight your unique strengths and capabilities? You told me a few weeks ago about how you solved a problem at work that no one else could figure out. That seems smart to me. I have a hunch you've shown some smart behaviors in a lot of other situations too.*

Step 6: Assign Homework Exercises

The client should continue logging the microaggressions they experience or witness and their thoughts and responses to them. Between this session and the next one, the client should also retake relevant symptom questionnaires to compare to baseline and ensure they are progressing. This would include the RTS or the TSDS, as well as any other self-report measures where the scores were in the clinical range. They can complete the measures right after this session, do them at home and bring them to session, or complete them online via your electronic medical record system.

Client readings in advance of the next session:

Norton, H. L., Quillen, E. E., Bigham, A. W., Pearson, L. N., & Dunsworth, H. (2019). Human races are not like dog breeds: Refuting a racist analogy. *Evolution: Education and Outreach, 12*(1), Article 17. https://doi.org/10.1186/s12052-019-0109-y

Williams, M. T. (2020, June 13). What is Whiteness? *Psychology Today*. https://www.psychologytoday.com/ca/blog/culturally-speaking/202006/what-is-whiteness

Sessions 6 and 7: Exposure and Processing of Experiences of Racism

In this stage, your client will overcome upsetting memories through the process of exposure and habituation. By having conversations about the distressing events with you, the client will be able to create new thinking patterns about the events, reducing the client's distress, shame, and guilt. This part of the treatment will require multiple sessions; repeat the following steps as many times as needed.

Step 1: Review Homework

Review the homework assignment by asking the client about the log of microaggressions they've been completing. Look for signs of growth around their observation and understanding of microaggressions, and offer praise for any evidence of an expanded perspective. Discuss the reading assignments, both the Williams (2002) and Norton et al. (2019) articles, and explore the client's reflections and emotions related to the readings. Make sure to collect the symptom questionnaires from the client, if not done already. If they have not completed them, use the first 10 minutes of the session for this purpose.

Step 2: Recounting Racism-Related Traumatic Experiences

Victims of racial trauma often avoid discussing their experiences with racism out of fear of that they will become emotionally overwhelmed and be unable to cope as a result. However, the reality is that, over the long term, recounting these unpleasant events will alleviate their symptoms of trauma, as exposure leads to habituation (i.e., a decrease in anxiety without the need for harmful safety and avoidance strategies), results in disconfirmatory learning (i.e., evidence that counters incorrect trauma-related beliefs), and provides opportunities to process and resolve those experiences. Therefore, exposure is a critical step in healing from racial trauma, so the material covered in this session will likely need to be extended to several sessions.

The goal is to help your client regain control of the past by being able to recount the trauma without feeling helpless. Recounting the trauma can be conceptualized as a form of storytelling, in which the client creates a narrative about their experience with key characters and a beginning, a middle, and an end. Storytelling facilitates an understanding of human behavior and can also be an important tool for resisting oppression and even promoting spiritual communion. To fight negative narratives about marginalized communities, storytelling has been used in community contexts to help restore cultural identities, foster a sense of belonging, and counter dominant narratives. As a result, therapeutic and community-building strategies based on the use of storytelling have been adopted as a reaction to racial trauma. To prepare clients for this next phase, you can say:

- *"Confronting the totality of your painful experiences is the only way to gain mastery over the past. It allows you to objectively revisit what happened so that you can reassess it from a safe and objective vantage point. It allows you to gain a more complete picture of the events and to come to more appropriate conclusions about the cause and meaning of what happened. This understanding allows you to move past the urge to avoid reminders of these experiences and allows you to create a better understanding of who you really are in a more useful and accurate way.*

- *"It will be hard to get started because you are probably afraid. That is totally normal. Just remember that the memory of what happened is only an imprint in your brain and not the actual event itself, so it is completely safe to revisit. You may feel stress when you do these exercises. You may cry or even feel disoriented for a short while. Be good to yourself and find as many excuses as you can to reward yourself later for pushing through it."*

There are several different types of exposure exercises based on storytelling that can promote healing, as detailed in the following steps. It is recommended that you try all of these, perhaps using one session to focus on each. However, you should understand that a key source of healing that undergirds all of these techniques is providing space for clients to fully express their pain and be heard. As a caring and supportive human being, bearing witness to your client's pain is itself a healing act, and perhaps the most healing thing you can do.

Step 3a: Recounting Racism-Related Traumatic Experiences with Imaginal Exposure

Imaginal exposure is a type of storytelling in which the client vividly revisits the traumatic event in their imagination in the presence of the therapist (Foa et al., 2007). The mechanism through which imaginal exposure helps clients recover from racial trauma is in changing inaccurate cognitive patterns and anxieties about the trauma that are maintained through avoidance behaviors. Recounting the trauma in a safe and supportive environment empowers the client by providing them with a greater sense of control over how they respond to trauma memories, ultimately leading to a reduction in symptoms.

It is important that people with racial stress and trauma are able to share a detailed account of their experience with you. This is the basis of prolonged exposure, which is one of the first-line treatments for PTSD. When it comes to the use of prolonged exposure for racial trauma, therapists can make culturally relevant adaptations to the treatment process by explicitly asking about race-related themes throughout treatment and then bringing those distressing aspects to the center of treatment during imaginal exposures.

For example, consider Joan, a 60-year-old Black woman who was traumatized from being accosted by police at a grocery store. She was falsely accused of stealing by the manager, taken out in handcuffs, and forcibly searched in public. You can inquire openly about the client's thoughts and feelings and how these fit into her racial identity in the context of the trauma. For example, you can ask, "Do you believe you were accused of stealing because you are Black? Do you think the store manager would have still called the police if you had been White?" You can also encourage the client to more openly express how she felt about her Blackness when she was confronted with the traumatic event: "What do you fear people were thinking as they watched this happen to a Black woman? Let's be sure to include this in your narrative."

During the imaginal exposure itself, you will act as a guide for the client as they recollect and recount the racism-related traumatic event. To begin, you will ask your client to recall the upsetting event in their mind. Then ask them to provide you with a comprehensive and detailed description of their traumatic incident in the first-person present tense, going from beginning to conclusion, and assess their anxiety throughout. With repeated recounting of the incident, their subjective levels of distress should decrease over time. Here are the overarching steps of imaginal exposure:

- Identify and review the client's most upsetting experiences of racism.
- Choose just one event to start with.
- Have the client tell the whole story of the event, from beginning to end.
- The client should close their eyes and recount the story in the present tense.
- Interrupt as needed to glean more details, especially surrounding the client's emotions and senses.
- Gently inquire as to the level of distress the client feels in recounting the details of the story. You can use a subjective units of distress scale here (SUDS), if appropriate, to ensure the story is not too stressful or too easy.
- Once the client is done, repeat a short summary of the story back the client.
- If there is time, have the client repeat the story again, adding more details.

As you listen to your client share their stories of pain and trauma, you may be impressed with their strength and resilience. Recognizing this resiliency can be a wonderful way to support the client in overcoming any feelings of inadequacy. However, keep in mind that even though clients may have displayed much strength, it does not mean that they are doing well. Focusing too much on strengths can be an empathic failure, as it can negate their experience of suffering. It might be worth reminding them that no one should have to be strong all the time.

Image credit: Tori Press (https://www.instagram.com/revelatori)

It is recommended that you record the part of the session where the client retells their trauma experience so the client can listen to it for 30 to 45 minutes each day to facilitate habituation. (Or you can have the client write about it for homework, as described in client exercise 4.4 later in this chapter.) If you are unfamiliar with the imaginal exposure technique, see Foa and colleagues (2007) for details of this process and seek out peer supervision for guidance.

Step 3b: Recounting Racism-Related Traumatic Experiences with Written Expression

Writing can be used as an alternative way for the client to recount their traumatic experiences. To do so, you can ask them to write freely about their deepest thoughts and feelings concerning the traumatic race-related incident they encountered. This can be done in session or preferably as homework (see client exercise 4.4). At home, it is recommended that they continue writing about the same experience for at least three days. They should bring the written account to therapy and read it aloud in session. Processing their written narrative in session is more effective in decreasing PTSD symptoms than independent expressive writing, as it gives a chance for you to provide feedback.

After discussing the client's written account of the trauma, ask them to prepare a new version of the story for homework, without looking at the previous version again. The client can repeat this process until recounting the event no longer causes distress. Clients who have a great deal of distress may do better if they start by only writing facts about their trauma and add emotions to their stories later. You can explain to the client:

> *"You can continue to develop your story at home as a part of your healing process. You can add more details and other important aspects as they come to you. When you are done, this can also become a vehicle for collective healing for your community. Sharing your story with others will contribute to your healing, when you are ready. Others who have suffered the way you have will see this can be overcome."*

In session 10, I talk more about storytelling as a means of empowerment. By sharing stories of overcoming adversity, the client can inspire others who may be facing similar challenges. While the client is not ready at this point to share their whole story widely, the knowledge that their story may eventually be used to help others in their community can be a motivating factor when facing the stress of recounting painful memories and experiences.

Step 3c: Recounting Racism-Related Traumatic Experiences with Creative Expression

People with racial trauma may benefit from activities that allow them to creatively express their emotions surrounding the trauma. Photovoice is one such therapeutic technique that uses photography as a means for clients to express and process their experiences. It has been used in various contexts where members of marginalized communities use photographs to construct narratives relating to experiences of adversity, such as racism or poverty. Photovoice has also been used to collect information and stories around racial trauma from Indigenous people to better understand their mental wellness needs by providing participants with cameras and empowering them to document the community's needs and resources based on their own experiences. Photovoice can help clients get in touch with their emotions through exposure to visual stimuli, which is followed by an opportunity to express their feelings about specific trauma reminders in a supportive environment, fostering a deeper exploration of their experiences and facilitating healing.

When using photovoice with clients, first suggest some trauma-related themes or prompts that encourage them to capture images representing their feelings, memories, or experiences related to their trauma. These assignments can be broad or specific, depending on the client's needs. For example, in the case of Joan, she might be encouraged to take a picture of the store where the event happened, the store manager's photo in the entry of the store, a police car, the items that spilled from her purse when she was searched, or other things that might be salient to her experience. She will come up with her own items to photograph as well.

To use photovoice with your client, ask them to use their cell phone over the next week to capture images that resonate with them in relation to the trauma. At the next session, they can present their photos to you. Encourage them to discuss the story behind each image, what it represents, and how it relates to their trauma. Your role is to facilitate and guide this discussion for a meaningful and supportive experience. Afterward, guide the client in reflecting on their photovoice journey. Discuss any insights gained, changes in perceptions, or feelings toward their trauma

Processing Racial Trauma with Photovoice

Therapist: *Joan, you said you've taken several photographs. I'd love to hear what you have to share about each of them. Which one would you like to start with?*

Joan: [Takes her phone and scrolls to a photograph of the grocery store.] *This store... It's where everything happened. Whenever I see it, I feel anxious and humiliated, like I'm reliving that moment of being falsely accused. Sometimes I drive a different way to work just to avoid seeing it.*

Therapist: *That's a powerful image, representing a significant moment of trauma. I'm so sorry. What's the next photo you have there?*

Joan: [Shows a photo of a police car.] *I never liked seeing these, but now, it's just fear. That day, seeing the police cars made me feel so powerless.*

Therapist: *It sounds like a profound change in perception, from dislike to real fear. What about this next picture?*

Joan: [Presents a picture of items from her purse scattered on the ground.] *This is from when they searched me. My things were just thrown around, my privacy completely violated. I felt so exposed.*

THERAPIST: *It's a visceral depiction of your loss of dignity and privacy. And this last photo, it seems deeply personal.*

JOAN: *I took a picture of my driver's license. This is significant for two reasons. On that day, I was so flustered, I struggled to find my license when the police asked. It was like I had to prove who I was while being treated like a criminal. And also, it represents my identity. In that moment, I was reduced to a stereotype, not seen as a person with a history, a family, a career. This license is me, my identity, something more than what they saw.*

THERAPIST: *I feel a weight on my heart looking at this. It's both a symbol of the struggle you faced that day and a reclaiming of your identity. How does it feel to share these images and their stories?*

JOAN: *It's tough, really tough. But it feels necessary, like I'm giving voice to what happened to me in a way that I couldn't with just words.*

Photovoice is just one form of expression clients can use to address their trauma. There are many other expressive art ideas clients can use process their trauma.

Using Expressive Art to Help Heal from Racial Trauma

Activities such as painting, sketching, singing, or dancing can also allow people suffering from racial trauma to process their emotions through movement and creative expression.

- **Painting:** Clients can use oils, acrylic paints, or watercolors to convey any emotions they have related to their racial trauma. The client's emotions, their struggles, or the path to healing are represented through the colors, shapes, and brushstrokes.
- **Sketching:** Clients can use a pencil or charcoal to create sketches of past or current racist encounters. Sketches can act as a tool, helping people capture and record their feelings and experiences.
- **Singing:** Clients can create and perform a song about their racial trauma. The lyrics may reflect the client's personal experiences, their aspirations, or cries for social reform.
- **Dancing:** Dancing allows clients to express themselves via movement, as is done in contemporary dance. With their body acting as a means of communication, they may choreograph a dance piece that narrates their experiences related to racial trauma.
- **Culinary arts:** Clients can create a baked good that illustrates their emotions and state of mind by decorating it accordingly with words and designs.

Step 4: Processing Racist Experiences

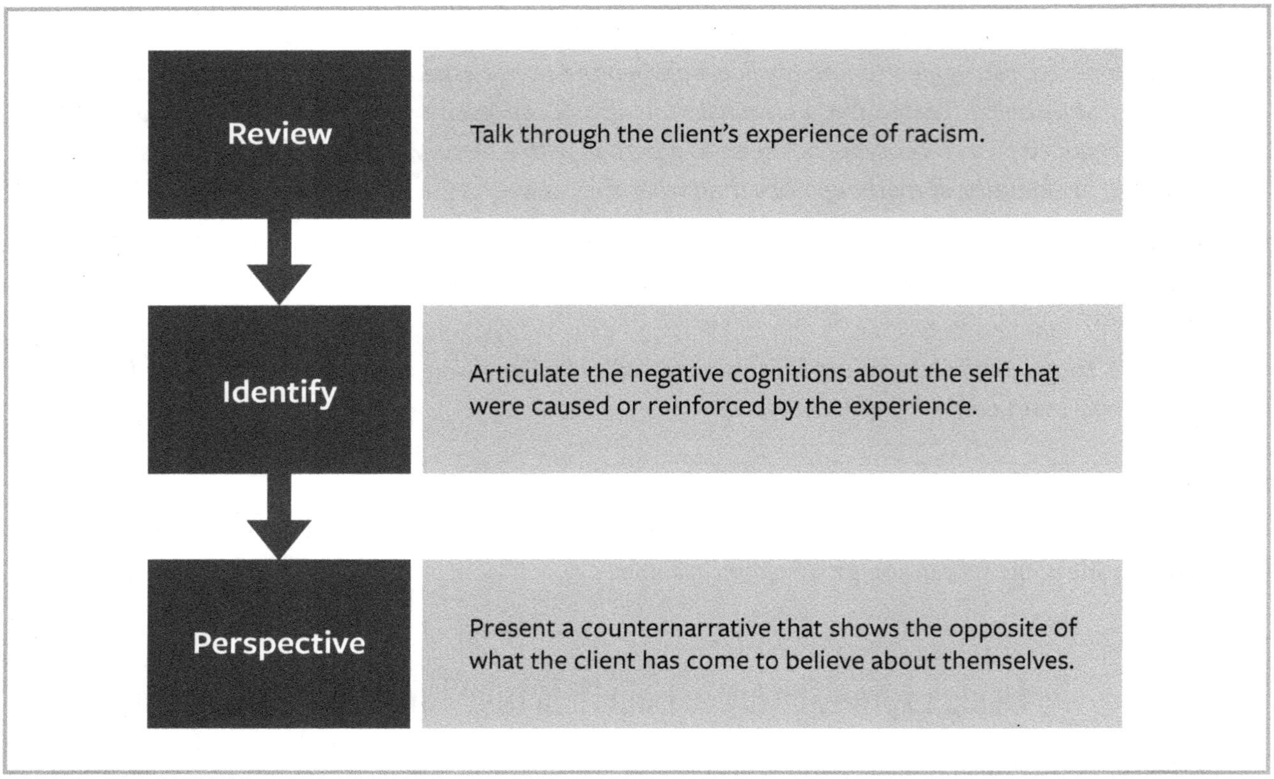

Review	Talk through the client's experience of racism.
Identify	Articulate the negative cognitions about the self that were caused or reinforced by the experience.
Perspective	Present a counternarrative that shows the opposite of what the client has come to believe about themselves.

Processing, which occurs after the client recounts their traumatic experience in the previous steps, allows the client to understand their experience from a more functional vantage point. As shown in the figure, it involves reviewing the trauma, identifying negative cognitions caused or reinforced by the experience, and helping provide an alternate, client-affirming perspective. This is vital for tackling feelings of shame, self-blame, and internalized racism. One helpful strategy in processing is to guide clients in externalizing racism by encouraging them to consider the broader context and intentions behind the racist actions rather than placing all the blame on themselves as "targets." By shifting the focus from individual "badness" to the systemic factors at play, clients can begin to heal and regain a sense of empowerment.

An important step here is to inquire openly about the client's thoughts and feelings regarding their racial identity in the context of their trauma. Some clients may even express self-criticism or make negative remarks about their ethnic or racial group. It's important to understand that these comments stem from their trauma experiences. Next, to alleviate the suffering associated with the client's memory of the experience, you can broaden the context, allowing the client to have a more objective and helpful perspective on what happened.

Here is where the use of Socratic questioning is helpful in pointing out cognitive distortions and false beliefs that the client may hold about the traumatic event, such as the belief that they are inadequate as a result of a traumatic incident. You can use this opportunity to point out individual strengths. For example, in the case of the Joan, you might say, "I am impressed with how courageous you were—to go back to the store and talk to the manager even though so much racism was present. What does this say about you?"

Socratic questioning allows the client to change their thinking about the distressing event, which in turn reduces distress, shame, and guilt.

Example of Socratic Questioning

Socratic questioning can be a powerful CBT technique for shifting a client's perspective. Here's an example of how a therapist might use Socratic questioning with a client in the context of reducing distress, shame, and guilt triggered by a workplace racial incident.

Therapist: *I understand that you're feeling a lot of distress and guilt about that incident at work. Let's explore it together. Can you tell me more about the part that made you so upset?*

Client: *Well, when I was in this meeting, someone made a super offensive comment about my race. I was frozen, so I couldn't say anything. I was just so embarrassed afterward.*

Therapist: *I see. Can you tell me more about what was said during the meeting?*

Client: *Sure, they made a joke about my accent and implied that I was a "diversity hire."*

Therapist: *Thank you for sharing that. That was not okay. Now, do you think this incident was solely about you, or could there be other factors at play here?*

Client: *I mean, it felt personal. They said those things right in front of me.*

Therapist: *I hear you. It's understandable to feel that way. However, let's consider this from a larger perspective. Do you think it is possible that this person's comments reflect a broader issue related to their own racial biases, rather than feelings about you as an individual?*

Client: *Well, yeah, I guess there might be a broader issue.*

Therapist: *That's an insightful observation. Keep in mind that harsh comments are just one manifestation of systemic racism, which is meant to put people of color in a subordinate position. Do you think it's fair to hold yourself responsible for the biases of others?*

Client: *No, when you put it that way, it doesn't seem fair at all.*

Therapist: *Exactly. Remember that the fact that you were the target of harsh remarks is not a reflection of who you are. Doesn't it seem more like the person being racist is the one with the problem?*

In this example, Socratic questioning encourages the client to explore the incident from a systemic perspective rather than placing sole blame on themselves. It helps the client recognize the broader context of racism and its impact, reducing feelings of shame and guilt while promoting empowerment and healing.

In addition to the use of Socratic questioning, you can point out the client's strengths when processing. For example, "It was very brave to press forth in a workplace where you endured so much harassment. How were you able to stay so productive for so long? What does this say about your ability to endure and your work ethic?"

Image credit: © Prostock-Studio; iStock

Consider another example, where a client talks about feeling helpless in the face of being racially profiled by police. He also berates himself for going to "that area of town" in the first place. You can help the client process this situation by saying something like:

> *"I'm sorry you had to endure such a horrifying experience. But you know, it's interesting how people who experience a trauma tend to blame themselves for things they have no control over. Since you were minding your own business, I don't see how you can think this was in any way your fault. How could you have known that the police would treat you that way? Where should we really be placing the blame?"*

You want to help clients process their traumatic experience by communicating racism and its impact in a non-paternalistic way, through open-ended questioning and compassionate, nonjudgmental listening, while maintaining a position of curiosity and humility.

Step 5: Assign Homework Exercises

Over the course of the next week, ask the client to continue doing the exposure exercises you practiced in session. They should be doing these exercises each day to continue the healing started in session. For clients who are processing their trauma through writing, you should assign the following exercise, which asks them to explore and process their trauma memories through journaling. Other weeks, the client might process their trauma by listening to the recording of their session daily, doing a photovoice activity, or engaging in creative expression. There are many ways to do exposure exercises to address trauma. As noted, repeated exposures to distressing memories are needed for healing, but they don't all have to be the same modality. However, it is important for the client to stick with exercises to experience habituation.

In addition to practicing exposure exercises, ensure that the client is continuing to engage in self-care, especially for this phase of the treatment. They should be doing something each day that includes exercise (even if only 15 minutes), an enjoyable activity, or a nourishing social connection.

Client reading in advance of the next session: Williams, M. T. (2017, September 4). Racism hides behind the small things people say and do. *Psychology Today*. https://www.psychologytoday.com/us/blog/culturally-speaking/201709/racism-hides-behind-the-small-things-people-say-and-do

Client Exercise 4.4

Healing Racial Trauma at Home: The Power of Writing

For this exercise, you will need your journal or a supply of paper, as well as some time and space where you can reflect and write about your experiences. When you are ready, begin by revisiting your earliest painful memory of racism and write about this event for at least 20 minutes. To best connect with the experience, write in the first-person present tense as if the event were happening now.

Start by determining the bookends of the experience—the beginning and end. Determine when you first realized that you were in an unjust, disempowered, or dangerous situation. At what point did you first start to feel anxiety or fear? What happened as your distress was increasing? How did the event unfold? What would you identify as the endpoint? When did you feel that you were safe, or that the distress of the situation began to decrease? Sometimes people hold in their feelings until later. If that happened for you, that is also okay—you will just include that in the story.

Write down everything you can remember about the experience and your thoughts at the time. For example, what did you think would happen? What did you wish would have happened instead? How did you interpret this event at the time (i.e., why did you think it happened)? How did it make you feel about yourself? Whom do you blame for what happened and why? (You can blame more than one person.) How do you feel toward the other people involved? How will this event affect you in the future? How does it affect how you feel about yourself today? How does it affect your relationships in the past and today? What sorts of things cause this memory to pop up for you?

After you have finished writing about this experience, walk away and give yourself a break. Later, revisit what you wrote, alone or with a supportive, trusted person. Think through the experience using your adult mind. How does the experience of revisiting it change your perception of the event? The next day, discard what you wrote, and write about the entire event again. Add more details if you can. As you repeat this process, observe how your perspective on the event shifts. What changes? What do you learn?

Share your story with a good friend or your therapist. Sharing your experience with another person is a good way to break the power of shame and help come to a quicker resolution from the pain.

When the memory no longer causes distress, start over again with another upsetting memory about racism. Keep doing this until you have gone through all your painful memories, or you are no longer feeling upset about your experience of racism. Getting through all your painful memories may take many weeks, so take your time. With perseverance and consistency, you will eventually get through it. And as the worst memories start to feel less upsetting, other similar memories will automatically start to lose their hold on you, so you may find you have fewer painful memories to process than you thought.

Session 8: Learning Strategies to Combat Racism

The main purpose of this session is to use tools like microinterventions, imagery rescripting, and role-playing to help the client build the skills needed to respond to racism across various situations and to increase their confidence to act.

Step 1: Review Homework

Begin by inviting the client to share their written narratives, making sure to encourage them to elaborate on any difficulties or insights they encountered when recalling a painful experience of racism. Ask them to express how they felt during the writing process and discuss what changes they observed in their perspective as they revisited the memory. Look for any changes in their emotional responses or self-perception as they reevaluate the event.

If the client shared their story with a friend, explore how this affected the client's emotional experience and their perception of the trauma memory. Evaluate the client's readiness to confront additional distressing memories and see if they feel less distressed about the experiences they've processed so far. This collaborative review process assists clients in processing their racial trauma and encourages them to continue on this transformative journey toward healing and growth.

Step 2: Building Skills to Confront Racism

Common sense tells us that the only way to overcome victimization is to resist being victimized. While this is not always possible, it often is. Nonetheless, traumatized clients typically have lost their ability to effectively confront racism, even when doing so entails little or no personal risk. They will need to be taught (or retaught) how to do this and eventually be encouraged to do so.

When clients are confronted with racism—whether as targets or observers—they face complex decisions about whether to speak up or remain silent. While racism exists everywhere, it should not be passively tolerated. Therefore, treatment for racial trauma should involve working with clients to empower them to make changes within their sphere of control, including helping them develop the skills and agency they need to respond effectively to these incidents. Some strategies you can use to equip people of color with the skills to address racism in the moment include microinterventions, imagery rescripting, and role-playing. These strategies focus either on educating the offender of racism or confronting the offensive behavior. As a note, at this stage in treatment, you will not be asking the client to respond to everyday racism just yet, but you should still engage in discussions with clients about various constructive ways they *could* respond to these experiences.

Microinterventions

The starting point is to introduce the concept of *microinterventions* as a possible response to microaggressions (Sue et al., 2019). A racial microintervention is a deliberate, small-scale action or comment aimed at countering racial biases, affirming racial and ethnic identities, and promoting inclusivity and equity in daily interactions. Unlike microaggressions, which are subtle statements or behaviors that unintentionally perpetuate racial stereotypes or biases, microinterventions deliberately and actively challenge those biases to create a supportive environment for racialized people. For example, if someone mistakenly attributes a person of Asian descent as being "good at math" based purely on racial stereotypes, a racial microintervention might involve another person saying, "Talent in math isn't race specific. Let's not generalize or stereotype here." This intervention not only corrects the bias but also educates offenders and bystanders about the dangers of racial generalizations.

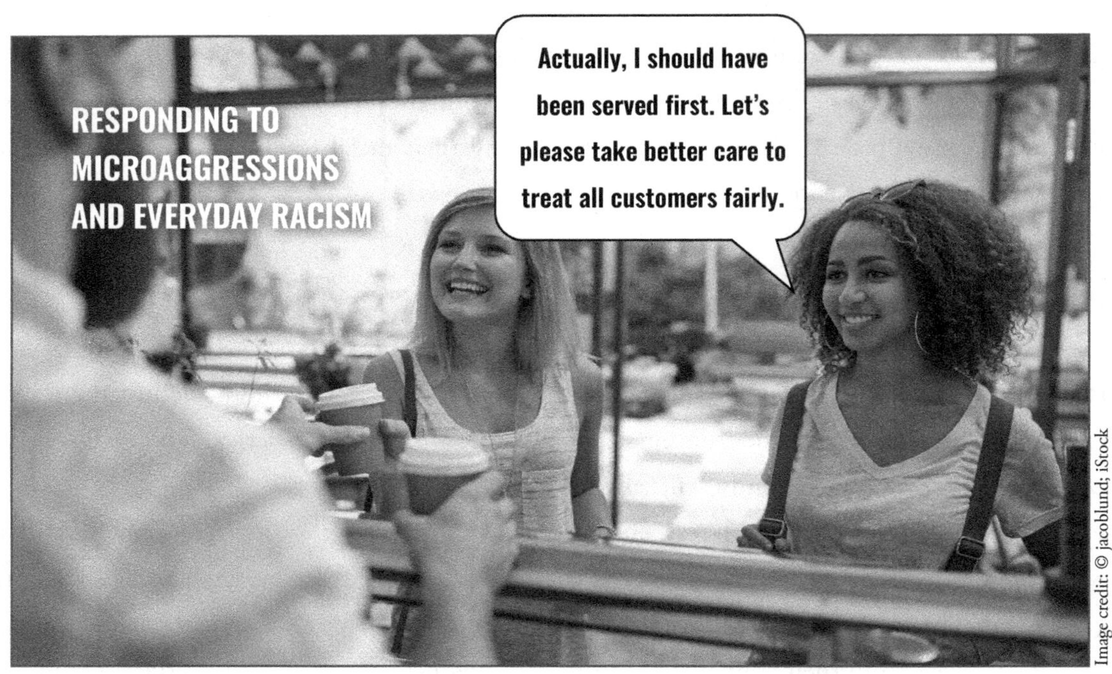

Image credit: © jacoblund; iStock

Likewise, targets of microaggressions can employ microinterventions to counteract the negative effects of the racist comment, educate the offender, and advocate for themselves. For instance, if a colleague says to a person of Latine heritage, "You speak English really well," implying that maybe they shouldn't because of their ethnicity, the individual might respond with a microintervention like "Thanks, you do too! By the way, I was born and raised in New York, so English is my first language." This response not only corrects the misconception but also subtly highlights the inappropriateness of the assumption, nudging the offender to reevaluate their biases.

Let the client know that although they should not yet implement this strategy, they can think about how a microintervention might help the next time someone commits a microaggression. How would they like to show up as the best possible version of themselves if they did not fear the outcome?

Imagery Rescripting

Another effective method that prepares clients to confront racism is imagery rescripting, in which the client confronts a distressing memory and reframes the racist encounter in a more empowering way. This allows the client to develop an alternative ending for an upsetting event they experienced in the past. The process of developing a different and preferred ending better prepares them to respond to such incidents in the future and is also a form of exposure. Even though the client knows the actual experience did not have this new ending, it is still helpful for resolving trauma.

To implement this technique, you ask the client to identify a specific memory related to racial trauma that is particularly distressing. It is essential to be specific to effectively work through the details of the event. You guide the client to vividly visualize the memory—recounting the events, feelings, thoughts, and bodily sensations tied to the memory. You then guide the client to imagine changing some aspect of the memory. This could involve the client standing up for themselves, a bystander intervening, the aggressor apologizing, or any other empowering modification. The objective is to reframe the event in a way that transforms the client's feelings of helplessness or distress into feelings of empowerment and control.

You then encourage the client to revisit the rescripted memory multiple times, which helps solidify the new, empowering narrative. Over time, the rescripted version will lessen the emotional distress tied to the original memory. The new ending will also help the client visualize and mentally rehearse a better way to respond to the incident, which will make it easier to respond in the same way should a similar racist event occur again. As a result, the client will be less afraid of such an event reoccurring because they will feel more prepared to act differently, and the repeated exposures to the memory will help them subsequently feel less triggered by reminders of the event.

After the imagery rescripting, discuss the experience with the client, exploring how they felt during the process and the differences between the original and rescripted memories. This discussion helps consolidate the therapeutic gains and facilitate greater insight.

Role-Play

To further assist clients in developing the courage and skills needed to confront racism, you can use in-session role-plays to rehearse real or potential situations where the client might encounter racial microaggressions or outright racism. Before engaging in role-plays, you should work with your client to collaboratively identify the emotions that these scenarios evoke and analyze how the client usually responds in such situations. This groundwork sets the stage for the role-plays you will do in session, where you take on the role of the aggressor or a bystander, and the client practices how to more effectively respond (see table 5.1 in the next chapter).

During these role-plays, you will provide a safe space for the client to experiment with various strategies, from using assertive communication to setting boundaries or even seeking support from allies. Offer real-time feedback, reinforcing the more effective behaviors and suggesting modifications where needed. As the client becomes more adept, the scenarios can be adjusted to increase complexity or emotional intensity.

The goal is not just to prepare the client to effectively manage racial confrontations but also to empower them with a sense of control and self-efficacy. Over time, as the client repeatedly enacts these rehearsed behaviors in the safety of the therapy room, they internalize the confidence and skills necessary to confront racism outside the therapeutic environment. This iterative practice helps clients move from a place of trauma-induced vulnerability to one of confidence and empowerment.

The Trauma of Police Violence and Aggression

When it comes to confronting racist events, one particular issue that deserves attention is whether or not it is appropriate for people of color to speak out against police violence and aggression. Unfortunately, American law enforcement has roots that date back to the times of slavery and colonization. Many southern police departments started as "slave patrols," aiding wealthy landowners in the retrieval and punishment of escaped slaves; these patrols are often cited as precursors to contemporary American law enforcement. The Black community's collective memory carries the weight of police abuses, spanning from the era of slave patrols, through the horrific instances of lynchings, to the violence faced by Civil Rights activists in the 1960s. Regrettably, these traumas persist today, as incidents of police brutality and the unjustified killing of unarmed people of color continue to occur.

Image credit: © Framestock Footages | Dreamstime.com

Moreover, racial biases are not limited to the Black community alone. Consider the case of Dr. David Dao, an Asian American lung specialist. He was forcefully removed and injured on a flight because he did not relinquish his rightfully purchased seat to an airline employee (see the client reading for this week). Despite the "model minority" stereotype often attributed to Asian Americans, which assumes them to be polite and deferential, Dr. Dao's mistreatment underscores that deviations from such stereotypes can result in harsh consequences even for otherwise respected medical professionals, echoing the racial biases and violence often experienced by Black and Latine communities in the US.

Consider also the plight of Indigenous peoples in Canada and the US, who have endured systemic discrimination, forced assimilation, and cultural erasure, predominantly through mechanisms like the residential school system. This historical trauma establishes a backdrop for their present-day interactions with law enforcement. The over-policing of Indigenous communities, coupled with high rates of incarceration, underscores a long-standing and ongoing mistrust between the police and these groups.

Therapists working with clients on issues of racial trauma should also be cognizant of the complexities surrounding police behavior, many of whom may themselves be dealing with trauma. A significant portion of law enforcement officers in North America are military veterans. After serving in combat zones, these veterans may return home with PTSD or other trauma-related conditions. When officers with untreated PTSD are placed in high-pressure situations, their heightened stress responses can lead to overreactions. Simultaneously, people of color, who are acutely aware of the historical and current disproportionate police violence against their communities, might respond to police presence with visible anxiety—sweating, avoidance of eye contact, or in extreme cases, attempts to flee. To an officer with PTSD, these signs of anxiety, though rooted in legitimate fear, might be misinterpreted as deceit or guilt, potentially escalating a situation.

This confluence of traumas—one stemming from the horrors of warfare and the other from historical and current systemic racial oppression—can create volatile encounters, making these confrontations life-threatening to citizens of color. In these situations, people of color are advised to stay calm and work to de-escalate the situation. However, in cases of police behaving badly, the client should be advised to lodge a complaint against the officer once they are in a safe location, even if they don't expect it will make a difference. The point is to practice pushing back against racism to increase feelings of agency to overcome fear, whether or not anything comes of the complaint.

Step 3: Determine If an Escape Plan Is Needed

Although a big part of healing from racial trauma involves teaching clients how to develop the confidence to combat racism in the future, if high levels of racism are regularly occurring in the client's environment, an escape plan becomes essential. In particular, the client may need to make major life changes to distance themselves from extreme racism.

Therefore, you should engage in a discussion to identify the major sources of racial trauma in the client's life and explore healthy strategies to reduce exposure to these sources. This may involve considering significant life changes, such as working from home, changing jobs or schools, ending a relationship, relocating to a new neighborhood, distancing from toxic friends, or limiting interactions with certain family members. While these decisions are not easy, they are sometimes necessary to create a space for healing and minimize exposure to racism, fostering the client's well-being and growth. You can facilitate this discussion by asking, "Would you say that racial trauma is ongoing for you at this point? If so, we may need to discuss an escape or exit plan for you."

Escaping highly damaging situations is not to be confused with avoidance, as clients will need to learn how to engage with everyday racial stressors. However, people do need to get themselves out of racially abusive situations.

Developing an Escape Plan

There is a difference between learning how to confront racism in a healthy manner versus continuing to get traumatized by high levels of racism that overwhelm your ability to cope. This exercise will help you develop an exit plan when the sources of racial trauma in your life remain an unacceptable and ongoing problem.

1. **Identify the stressor.** Describe the situation causing ongoing racial trauma for you.

____

____

____

2. **Assess the need.** List all the ways the high levels of racism associated with this situation are impacting your well-being.

____

____

____

____

____

____

3. **Brainstorm strategies and decide.** Think about some strategies to eliminate the exposure to this specific stressor. Consider changes like working from home, changing jobs or schools, relocating, or distancing yourself from a toxic individual by limiting interactions with them or ending the relationship. Don't prejudge any ideas—your ideas can be radical, out-there, or different. They may seem impractical at first, and that's okay. For each idea, list the potential benefits and difficulties.

____

____

____

____

____

____

4. **Create your escape plan.** Pick an idea and utilize the template below.

   - **Goal:** ____

     ____

     ____

   - **Action steps:** ____

     ____

     ____

   - **Timeline:** ____

     ____

     ____

   - **Support system:** ____

     ____

     ____

5. **Review and adjust.** Review your ideas with your therapist. Discuss which plan you chose and why. You can adjust your escape plan if needed.

Step 4: Assign Homework Exercises

Encourage clients to continue recording instances of microaggressions using the *Microaggressions Log*, including how the event went and how they wish they had responded. In addition, review the concept of developing an escape plan, whether it's needed now or in the future in case racism escalates. Ask the client to make their own tentative escape plan and to discuss how they can overcome barriers to its implementation.

Client reading in advance of the next session: Williams, M. T. (2017, April 29). Unfriendly skies: United Airlines and police violence. *Psychology Today*. https://www.psychologytoday.com/us/blog/culturally-speaking/201704/unfriendly-skies-united-airlines-and-police-violence

Learn more (for therapists and clients who would like a more in-depth reading): Sue, D. W., Alsaidi, S., Awad, M. N., Glaeser, E., Calle, C. Z., & Mendez, N. (2019). Disarming racial microaggressions: Microintervention strategies for targets, White allies, and bystanders. *American Psychologist, 74*(1), 128–142. https://doi.org/10.1037/amp0000296

Part 3—Empowerment

Your clients have come a long way on their healing journey, and they're now ready to take their empowerment to the next level. This chapter delves into strategies for practicing valued actions, fostering posttraumatic growth, and taking meaningful steps toward racial justice. It's a pivotal moment in the journey toward healing and empowerment.

In chapter 5, you will:

- Guide your client in practicing how to address racism in their daily experiences.
- Help the client consolidate their experiences into a cohesive and meaningful narrative.
- Encourage the client to evaluate their values, navigate challenging situations, and work toward racial justice goals.
- Synthesize the treatment process.
- Empower the client with techniques for relapse prevention and resilience.

Chapter Overview

In this chapter, you will shift your focus to the empowerment phase of the healing journey. By this point, your clients have progressed significantly in their understanding of racial trauma, coping strategies, and support networks. Now it's time to harness this newfound strength and translate it into tangible action.

To do so, you'll explore techniques to help your client actually confront racism in their daily life. Building on these experiences, you'll then guide them in consolidating these events into a cohesive and meaningful narrative. This process facilitates posttraumatic growth, allowing the client to find deeper meaning and purpose in their journey. Furthermore, the client will learn how to evaluate their values, navigate challenging situations, and work toward racial justice goals. This empowers them to continue making meaning of their past trauma, drive change in their environment, and feel a sense of agency in the broader context of social action and activism. As the final step, you'll bring together the tools and insights gained throughout the treatment process. The client will leave this phase prepared to navigate the road ahead with newfound resilience and be empowered to create positive change in their life and community.

Session 9: Combating Racism in Everyday Life

When victims of racial trauma are able to respond directly to acts of racism, they can reclaim their voices in a powerful way. This session is focused on practice using these skills in vivo. Repeat it as many times as needed for your client.

"Courage is the most important of all the virtues because without courage, you can't practice any other virtue consistently."
–Maya Angelou

Image credit: Soph Jackson (https://www.instagram.com/turquoisemagpie)

Step 1: Review Homework

Review the client's *Microaggressions Log* and explore how they felt about reflecting on these experiences and recording them. Were there any specific insights or patterns that emerged? Ask the client to share their thoughts on how they wished they had responded to these microaggressions. Encourage them to discuss any challenges or barriers they may have identified in responding assertively.

Next, discuss the client's escape plan, addressing any ideas they came up with and their feelings about the plan. What reactions or feelings came up for the client while creating the escape plan? Did they find it empowering or challenging? Offer support and guidance if they encountered any difficulties or uncertainties while creating the plan. Help them refine it if needed.

Last, discuss the reading assignment and its relevance to their experiences. Explore any emotional reactions the client may have had while reading the article and how it may have influenced their perspective on their racial trauma. It is common for clients to feel anxiety, fear, or even disgust in reaction to the articles.

Step 2: Confronting Racism

When confronted with racism, both targets and observers must decide whether to speak up or remain silent. This decision is influenced by many factors, including the potential risks involved (e.g., losing a job), whether the individual's basic needs have been met (e.g., if they are too sick, tired, or hungry to effectively stand up for the issue in the moment), and what their emotional state is at the time (e.g., their initial response might be shock, which may limit their ability to think through what to say or do in the moment). In order to decrease the impact of racism, your client will need to start responding to these events constructively. When a victim of racial trauma learns to respond directly to acts of racism, it empowers them to reclaim their voice, challenge discrimination, and change their reality. This will allow them to develop a strong sense of personal agency, which can promote healing in the face of racism. People feel more empowered when they have greater control over how they respond to racist incidents.

One question people often have is how exactly they should respond to microaggressions. The table on the next page illustrates how a client should (and should not) respond when they witness or experience a racist incident (Williams, Holmes, et al., 2023). You should review this in detail with your client and also provide a copy for their reference.

Table 5.1 How to Respond to Microaggressions and Other Acts of Racism

1. Caring family member or close friend	
DO: ▪ Share your feelings and explain how the racist act affected you. ▪ Appeal to the strength of your relationship to foster mutual understanding, growth, and change.	**DO NOT:** ▪ Avoid the conversation. Sweeping the issue under the rug may strain your relationship over time. It's better to address the microaggression rather than ignore it.
2. Coworker or acquaintance	
DO: ▪ Politely educate the person about stereotypes and racism. ▪ Empower yourself to take positive action against racism while maintaining your personal integrity.	**DO NOT:** ▪ Respond to the person with anger or hostility. Hostile reactions can lead to further conflict and may hinder productive communication. ▪ Expect they will immediately appreciate the education. But over time, repeated messaging may help them make more inclusive choices.
3. Stranger	
DO: ▪ Be assertive and correct the person. ▪ Reject any attempts to control the encounter. ▪ Reclaim your agency and publicly resist racism.	**DO NOT:** ▪ Put yourself in danger. While being assertive is encouraged, don't put yourself in a physically unsafe situation. Prioritize your safety and well-being.
4. Powerful person in a dangerous situation	
DO: ▪ Remove yourself from the situation as quickly as possible. ▪ Report the incident to the authorities (even anonymously if necessary), even if you don't expect a useful outcome. This practice helps you assert your agency.	**DO NOT:** ▪ Respond directly to the act of racism. ▪ Expect the system to change overnight, but continue to assert your agency when necessary. Understand that reporting to authorities may not lead to an immediate resolution.

While discussing these possible responses, it is important to respect a client's fear or hesitancy to confront racism, especially if you are a therapist with a non-stigmatized identity. When clients have racial trauma, it will almost always feel unsafe to confront someone about their racism, even in small ways and when they are likely quite safe. Usually, their traumatization will have resulted in some level of avoidance of feared people and situations, which can be counterproductive. The client must learn to take calculated risks to increasingly venture outside of their comfort zone, whenever possible, and expose themselves to these situations. This process is similar to in vivo exposure, a core component of prolonged exposure.

Further, some means of addressing racism in the moment will be better received by certain offenders than others. It is important to keep in mind that for the client, the goal is not to "stop people from being racist" or even to "educate other people," although we can certainly hope for these outcomes. The more central goal is to facilitate the client's ability to tolerate discomfort in the service of being their authentic selves in the moment, which cannot occur unless they are empowered to use their voice in a manner that is fitting to their personality and values.

For example, a case study of an Asian American student seeking therapy for racial trauma discussed how the student was distressed about ongoing microaggressions from his friends (Ching, 2022). The therapist framed the action of speaking up against microaggressions as a values-driven, autonomous exposure that the client could try, and for which he subsequently reported success. For instance, the client pointed out to his roommates the racially insensitive comments they had made about peaceful Black Lives Matter protests in their town, which led them to apologize. This later sparked a deep conversation about race in America that ultimately brought them closer together.

Step 3: Interventions

As a clinician, you must encourage your client to embrace courage, while acknowledging the importance of safety, when confronting racism head-on. That's because when a client speaks up in the face of a racist incident, there are inherent risks involved, such as the possibility of retaliation from the perpetrator. Therefore, it is important to help your client discern between situations that are objectively dangerous and those that are merely uncomfortable. By equipping your client with the ability to make these distinctions, they can navigate these challenging scenarios with greater confidence and awareness.

Maintaining this balance between safety and courage is a delicate but necessary part of healing from racial trauma. If a client consistently prioritizes "safety" by avoiding confrontation or difficult conversations, this can inadvertently contribute to ongoing traumatization. In many cases, it's the avoidance of these challenging situations that maintains and exacerbates the trauma. For that reason, clients must step out of their comfort zones when confronting racism. This doesn't mean recklessly disregarding safety, but rather adopting a stance where they can assert themselves and address racism head-on, taking back their voice and power in the face of racial adversity.

Therefore, in this phase, you will help your client take valued actions to combat racist behavior *when it is safe* rather than being a passive victim. Remember that, at times, it may not be safe to confront someone who is committing a microaggression (e.g., an armed police officer who is engaging in racial profiling). Rather, you are helping the client learn adaptive responses that will ideally come to replace maladaptive strategies. You have already worked on this in prior sessions, but you can use hypothetical modeling or more role-play scenarios to demonstrate adaptive responding to certain scenarios. For instance, the following are strategies to speak up when a microaggression occurs rather than going along with it (Yoon, 2020):

- **Asking for more clarification:** "Please say more about what you mean by that" or "What makes you think that is true?"
- **Separating intent from impact:** "I know you didn't realize this, but when you said ______, it was hurtful because ______. Instead, you could say ______."
- **Sharing your own process:** "Based on what you said, it seems that you think ______. I used to think that too, but then I learned ______."
- **Showing it is not appropriate or wanted:** "Come on, let's not go there." Or use nonverbal communication such as shaking your head or making a grimace.

Image credit: © curtoicurto; iStock

Consider this example from a Native American client named Stephanie, who was humiliated in front of her coworkers at a staff meeting. After proving support and validation, you could suggest the following alternate response:

> *"That was horribly racist, and there is no excuse for it. But let's use this as a way to think about how to respond so you don't feel so disempowered next time this happens. How would it be to say something like this: 'I'm sure you meant that to be funny, but can we stop for a moment and think about why that might actually be a hurtful thing to say to a Native American person?'"*

One principle underlying the previous statements is helping the aggressor understand that they are not under attack for their comment. While this is a good principle to use when responding to microaggressions perpetrated by friends and colleagues, clients don't need to be friendly or expend emotional labor trying to educate or coddle someone whose comments are not well-intended, especially if the person is a stranger. A client should push back when microaggressions are hostile. Remember, microaggressions are an aggressive power play where the perpetrator is asserting inappropriate dominance over the target, whether or not the perpetrator recognizes this. The perpetrator's behavior should not be positively reinforced, or it will continue. To help your client prepare for this, you can help them brainstorm some of the most common microaggressions they experience and role-play how to respond. You could even use humor. For example:

AGGRESSOR: *Why are you wearing that towel thing on your head?*

CLIENT: *Why are you wearing that ugly T-shirt from the dollar store?*

AGGRESSOR: *Why is* that *your name?*

CLIENT: *I could ask you the same question. Why is your name Rob? You gonna rob a bank?*

As noted, the type of response will vary based on the relationship between the client and the perpetrator, as that dictates the level of vulnerability appropriate for the situation. For example, if a client is having tamales for lunch, and someone makes a joke about their choice of food, their response may differ as follows:

- **Caring family member or close friend:** Share how it made you feel and why. "It's actually hurtful when you joke about my cultural food like that. When I was kid, I was teased at lunchtime for eating these kinds of foods, and it brings back sad memories for me."
- **Coworker or acquaintance:** Gently educate the person about stereotypes and racism. "Well, look at what you brought for lunch, microwave pizza. You know that shitty processed food is full of chemicals and will kill you. This is actually wholesome and delicious, so don't be that way."
- **Stranger:** Be assertive and correct the person; reject any controlling aspects of the encounter. "Why are you so obsessed with what I'm eating? It's none of your business. Don't be a racist."

Image credit: © Creative Commons Zero (CC0); Dreamstime

In addition, you will want to prepare the client and let them know that some people will never change. Many are resistant to questioning their everyday experience, unfortunately. These individuals may react defensively and angrily. You might say:

> *"If the person you are confronting becomes emotionally reactive, try your best not to respond in the same way and to remain calm. Recognize that because you are reclaiming your power, the aggressor feels threatened and is becoming angry. This is not your fault, and you have no responsibility for making them feel better."*

Above all, remember that by practicing how to respond to racism in a productive manner, your client is a learning new behavior, and they cannot be expected to get it right every time. If they fall short, or make a mistake, remind them that their number one priority is self-compassion. They must be able to forgive themselves (or the oppressors win!).

When Emotions Are High

Image credit: © fizkes; iStock

The client should consider not responding right away to racism when either the client or the aggressor is very emotional, especially if there are no trusted people around for support.

The client will almost always feel some emotion, and this can be important data. But they must feel centered and in control for an optimal response. If the client is highly agitated, they should take a break and revisit the matter later with a clear mind.

Step 4: Assign Homework Exercises

Thus far, your client has been keeping a *Microaggressions Log* to track their regular encounters with microaggressions and other forms of racism. Now, it is time for them to start confronting these racist incidents as they occur in real time. Because of all their practice logging these, they should now be able to quickly identify them. Over the next week and beyond, your client should confront all experiences of racism, no matter who perpetrates it, given that the manner of confrontation will differ based on who commits it. After each situation, they should use their empowerment journal to keep track of what they did in each case of racism, what worked and what did not, and what they would do differently next time. There may be times they are unable to do anything or don't realize what is happening until it is too late. This provides an opportunity to exercise self-compassion and just resolve to respond to the next racist incident.

Prior to engaging in this work, remind your client to review table 5.1 to ensure that their responses to microaggressions are safe and appropriate. Encourage them to also lean on their social support system to process these experiences as they arise.

Client reading in advance of the next session: Yoon, H. (2020, March 3). How to respond to microaggressions. *The New York Times.* https://www.nytimes.com/2020/03/03/smarter-living/how-to-respond-to-microaggressions.html

Session 10: Posttraumatic Growth and Meaning-Making

Meaning systems inform our understanding of ourselves and our lives, direct our personal goals, and contribute to a sense of well-being and life satisfaction. This section is focused on facilitating posttraumatic growth, which is a key objective in treating racial trauma. Here, you will help the client identify the meaning they have come to ascribe to the traumatic events and what they have learned. Storytelling can be an important way to distill meaning from the trauma by consolidating the client's experience of healing, growth, and empowerment into a cohesive narrative.

Step 1: Review Homework

Review with the client how they responded to microaggressions, processing what worked, what did not, and what the client might do differently next time. Encourage the client to persist, and help troubleshoot situations that did not go well.

Step 2: Posttraumatic Growth and Meaning-Making

In treating racial trauma, one big goal is to help clients experience positive changes in their lives after going through difficult times, a process called *posttraumatic growth*. It involves helping the client adjust to how they understand the world after a traumatic experience and finding new meaning. It means adjusting to difficult changes and having new tools to deal with challenges. Clients who can find meaning in challenging situations by creating more positive perspectives tend to cope better with future stress. Therefore, when your client starts feeling less upset and more in control of racism-related challenges, that's a good time to talk about posttraumatic growth and explore what their experiences mean to them.

In terms of meaning-making, you can introduce the idea that painful experiences are often quite terrible when we are going through them, but they can ultimately lead to growth and make us stronger and more empathetic toward others who suffer. Experiences of racism may also lead the client to acquire useful and valuable knowledge. Reflecting on these experiences is an opportunity to promote healing by focusing on what was learned. To introduce this idea, you might say:

> *"What would you say you have learned from these difficult experiences of racism you've shared with me over the past several weeks? What do you think are the key takeaways, and what stands out for you?"*

Even if no identifiable benefits emerged from the trauma experience, the survival and recovery of the client is a victory worth celebrating. The story has a happy ending because the client learned how to survive, heal, and thrive in a society where the odds were stacked against them. You might express this to the client as follows:

> Client: *I know I've come a long way, but I just don't see anything positive that came out of those experiences.*

Therapist: *It can be hard to see anything good coming out of something that caused so much pain and heartache. But you survived it, and now you are healing. It's a remarkable achievement. The people who did this to you wanted to put you in your place and keep you down. It didn't work. You're on your feet again. In facing and overcoming challenges, you've come out stronger and wiser. I know there is still some pain. But the victory lies in your ability to keep getting back up, despite the odds stacked against you.*

Meaningful works of art, music, or poetry that have emerged from their experiences can be tangible and positive reminders of the growth process.

Important Signs of Posttraumatic Growth

- Greater appreciation for life
- Improved relationships
- Enhanced personal strengths
- Changes in priorities
- Deeper spiritual connection
- Greater emotional resilience
- New perspectives and insights
- Willingness to help others
- Increased creativity
- Sense of inner growth and healing

Another strategy for fostering posttraumatic growth involves celebrating racial identity through activities that create meaning. These activities might involve learning how others from similar racial or ethnic backgrounds made sense of the racism they faced and achieved success despite obstacles. For example, someone might choose to engage in open discussions about race with their grandchildren, using this as an opportunity to affirm the beauty of their dark skin. This can lead to closer relationships, as the grandchildren turn to them for support when they encounter racism. The close bond formed in this way can help the person find meaning in their racial trauma—realizing that their experiences have motivated them to empower their grandchildren and instill a sense of pride in their distinctive look and heritage. The conversation might look something like this:

Client: *I've been thinking a lot about my racial identity. It's been challenging, but I want you to know I am hearing this—everything you've been teaching me. And I am learning to make peace with my experiences.*

Therapist: *That is so wonderful to hear. This inner transformation is a such beautiful part of your healing.*

Client: *There's an annual cultural festival in my community that I used to attend as a child. I have been avoiding it lately, but I decided I want to take my grandchildren. I want them to see how we celebrate our traditions and more people who look like they do.*

Therapist: *Fantastic! By finding ways to share your culture with your grandchildren, you're strengthening your bond with them and also helping them grow in self-esteem and confidence around their heritage and their beauty. It's wonderful to pass on this sense of pride and self-acceptance.*

CLIENT: *Yes, I think so too.*

THERAPIST: *I love how you're turning such a painful experience into a connecting experience. I hear a very hopeful future here.*

Additionally, racial trauma can cause people to have a crisis of faith or feel confused about their beliefs, as trauma can impact a person's sense of spirituality. Therefore, when helping your client make meaning after trauma, it is important to support them in strengthening and exploring their spiritual beliefs. As part of this process, you certainly respect their belief system and incorporate resources and interventions that align with their worldview. These may include religious rituals that symbolize the transition from a traumatized life to a renewed and more meaningful life. Such rituals can vary widely between cultures, from communal prayers and novenas to religious festivals like posadas and peregrinations. In some traditions, practices like baptism or lent serve as visible symbols of inner transformation. Regardless, these rituals can help your client grow beyond their traumatic experiences and also thrive—finding purpose, forming new relationships, and maintaining a positive outlook despite the challenges of racism.

At this point in the treatment process, you likely already know a little about your client's belief systems and worldviews, so you can ask them what would be a meaningful way to commemorate your time together, and if it would make sense to tie this into a ritual that has meaning to them.

"As we've been working together, I've noticed how deeply your experiences have affected not just your emotions, but perhaps your inner being as well. Trauma can sometimes shake our beliefs or make us question our faith. I'm wondering, how has your healing journey intersected with your spiritual beliefs or practices?"

[Client responds with their experience or perspective.]

"Your spiritual journey is a key part of who you are, and it can be a source of strength and meaning, especially after going through a trauma. Many find comfort and healing in rituals or practices from their faith or spiritual tradition. Have you thought about any rituals or practices that might help you as you move forward from here? I'm also thinking about ways we can mark this transformation for you. It's a significant moment."

Turning Pain into Art and Trauma into Gold

Image credit: © Marco Montalti; iStock

Like the golden cracks in pottery seen in the Japanese ceramic artform kintsugi, in trauma healing past harms are incorporated rather than erased, allowing the client to integrate their experiences to eventually become the golden edges of a unique new chapter in their life.

Step 3: Storytelling

Healing from racial trauma often involves retelling the trauma story from a perspective of healing, growth, and empowerment. Storytelling is especially culturally congruent with many clients of color and is a several-thousand-year-old tradition valued in many cultures around the world. Sharing their experiences not only promotes individual healing but also empowers communities and fosters racial solidarity.

To introduce the concept of storytelling to your client, explain that creating a story they tell themselves and share with others when they are ready can be a good way to process pain and promote self-healing. Storytelling is an effective tool for remembering and retelling something that has happened to us.

> *"We can develop your story in this session as a part of your healing process. This can also be a vehicle for collective healing within your community if you like. Others can learn based on what you have been through. Sharing your story will also contribute to your healing, if and when you are ready."*

In helping the client develop their story, here are some questions you can ask them to get the process started:

- *What is your story about?*
- *How would you tell your story?*
- *Would the story you tell your loved ones be different from the story you tell yourself?*
- *Whom is the story for?*
- *What is the beginning about?*
- *How does it end?*
- *Who are the characters involved?*
- *Is it a story of victory and triumph? A story of resilience?*
- *What is the moral of the story or lesson learned?*
- *What have you lost? What have you gained?*
- *How have you changed and grown through the process?*

Then spend the remainder of the session allowing the client to begin crafting their story. The client might start with a rough outline and then start filling in the details, or they might rework something they have already written as part of their healing process. This version will be written to share with trusted others, and although it is not required that the client share it outside of the session, it should be encouraged. The more the client can share their story with others, the more healing they will experience. Check in as needed to assist with the story, letting the client know that it is not expected that they complete it in session. Three to four pages is the typical length for clients' stories.

As a note, if there is any legal action happening surrounding the client's particular trauma experience, they may be considering a settlement agreement, which typically includes stipulations that prevent the client from sharing their story with others. Their own lawyers may even encourage this course of action, not understanding how damaging it can be for the client's voice to be stifled. Therefore, if the client is in the midst of legal action, they should be discouraged from agreeing to a non-disclosure agreement about their personal experience, as this robs the client of their voice, which can impede healing.

Step 4: Assign Homework Exercises

Encourage the client to complete and formalize their story and come into the next session with their full story to share with you, including how they have grown through the process. Encourage the client to celebrate writing their story in a small way once they complete it.

> **Client reading in advance of the next session:** Cooper, C. (2017, August 18). To the therapist who called me a "strong Black woman." *The Mighty*. https://themighty.com/topic/depression/therapy-racial-bias-strong-black-woman

Session 11: Social Action and Activism

This session will focus on using the knowledge and growth that the client has gained as a vehicle to bring about change in the client's environment. It is also a time for you and the client prepare for the end of your sessions together.

Step 1: Review Homework

Start by inviting the client to share their full story, emphasizing the importance of this step in their healing journey. Encourage them to reflect on any challenges or insights they encountered while formalizing their narrative, and ask if (and how) they celebrated their writing achievements. Inquire how they are feeling related to this process.

Next, delve into their reading of Candace Cooper's (2017) article and ask them to share their thoughts and reactions. Encourage them to draw connections or comparisons between the article and their own mental health care experiences.

Step 2: Introduce Termination

Introducing the idea of termination with your client represents a delicate and vital aspect of the therapeutic process. Begin by acknowledging the progress and growth that the client has achieved throughout their journey, placing emphasis on their newly acquired coping skills. Then encourage them to reflect on their goals, their milestones, and the positive changes they have experienced. Share your observations and insights regarding their progress to validate their efforts.

Next, have an open and honest conversation with your client about the transition out of therapy. To prepare them for termination, discuss how and when therapy will end. Let them know that their progress and their ability to achieve their therapeutic goals are the main reasons for concluding therapy. Assure them that the end of therapy does not mean the end of their personal growth journey; rather, it marks a transition to a more self-reliant phase. You might say:

> *"You have done so much great work in these sessions with me. I know some of this has been difficult, and I appreciate you for being so courageous and vulnerable with me. Next week is our last weekly meeting, so let's talk about some ways you can continue to combat systemic racism, process your own racial trauma, and promote self-healing and collective healing within your community now that our time together is ending. In the session to come, we'll discuss this more. This transition is a testament to your progress and readiness to take on new challenges."*

Step 3: Calling Attention to Social Action and Activism

Once clients have experienced a certain degree of healing, it is natural for them to consider activities they can do that promote social change to reduce injustice in their environment. Indeed, engaging in strategies to create positive change marks the final step in addressing racial trauma. These strategies can include advocating for anti-racist policies, participating in petition drives, exercising one's right to vote, educating others about racism, and, when necessary, pursuing legal actions against wrongdoers. The following are among some of the techniques described in the literature that can foster resistance and the prevention of racial trauma (Mosley et al., 2021):

- **Sharing one's story broadly:** Sharing narratives, critiques, experiences, blogging, etc.
- **Artivism:** Using creative art to advocate for liberation
- **Physical resistance:** Putting one's body at risk to defend, free, or affirm people of color
- **Organizing:** Designing objectives, defining results, and selecting tactics for anti-racism work
- **Teaching:** Educating people and encouraging them to continue learning about anti-racism and de-colonizing approaches
- **Coalition-building:** Creating, maximizing, and sustaining connections
- **Modeling/mentoring:** Connecting with another person of color on a one-on-one basis to confirm, support, and enhance collective health
- **Scholar activism:** Participating in and contributing to social change informed by academic research
- **Spacemaking:** Creating physical or virtual venues for people of color to gather to heal, organize, and celebrate
- **Community activism:** Addressing structural racism in areas like housing, work, and education through community gardens, tutoring programs for youth, support for businesses owned by people of color, workshops addressing racism in schools, etc.

Artivism Through Baking

Image credit: Rehman Abdulrehman

This cake was created for a national baking competition to draw attention to the impact of racism on a person's psyche, whereby they may look happy (colorful) on the outside but feel dead (colorless) on the inside.

Projects like this can be used to raise awareness and advocate for change, or they can simply be private activities used to help process the stress and trauma of experiences of racism.

These strategies enable survivors of racial trauma to collectively cope, heal, build connections, and engage in system-focused liberatory actions. Therefore, you should actively encourage your client to think about how they can promote racial justice and address racism through social engagement. Consider what forms of activism and resistance align with the client's values and are accessible to them, making sure to stress that there isn't a single "right" way to do this. By this point, most clients will already have ideas about what they want to see changed in their environments, and some will have already started on this path. You can ask your client if they're already active in social causes and, if not, discuss what kinds of activities they might be interested in.

You can also help your client identify ways to contribute based on their strengths and resources. For example, some clients may not want to attend protests but could help by creating promotional materials for demonstrations. Others may not have much time for coalition-building but could make a financial contribution to certain organizations. You can also explore whether your client has specific goals, like reducing racial profiling in their community or addressing microaggressions at their workplace, and help them set specific, achievable steps toward reaching those goals. For example, you might say:

> *"I want to emphasize that there are many ways to make a positive impact. It's all about finding what resonates with you. What kinds of activities or causes are most important to you? What are you particularly passionate about? Let's take a moment to consider your strengths and resources. For instance, if you like to attend protests, that is one way to advocate, and you can attend to show your support, but if that does not resonate with you, maybe you have skills that could be used to create promotional materials for demonstrations. Or perhaps you're limited on time but have the means to make a financial contribution toward causes you care about. We can brainstorm ways that align with your situation and abilities."*

Clients should understand that activism can take various forms and doesn't always involve formal protests or large events. They can explore opportunities to promote anti-racist change in their personal environments, such as their workplace, school, or community, through various prosocial means, like participating in committees to improve fair hiring practices.

> *"What are some things in your community that you would like to see changed? How else can you contribute? For example, you can arrange to give an anti-racism talk where you speak in front of an audience about your personal experiences of racism. You can also post on social media about anti-racism issues."*

In cases where your client has experienced institutionalized racism, such as media portrayals or biased educational curricula, they may feel particularly powerless to effect change. In such instances, you should collaborate with clients to explore meaningful ways to combat these problems.

> *"Many companies, schools, and institutions have racist policies. You can be a voice and help to change these kinds of policies. For example, in my state there was a problem of not enough licensed*

psychologists to meet the needs of everyone, particularly communities of color. And, at the same time, there were many immigrant mental health professionals who were qualified but unable to practice due to overly strict rules about foreign degrees not being accepted by the licensing board. I joined the state licensing board and formed an ad hoc committee to examine the issues. In the next year, we were able to implement some procedural changes that got rid of a lot of racist red tape and increased the licensure of foreign applicants fivefold. It was a real victory for everyone, and it led to more mental health professionals available to work in communities of color. How can you work toward change? Let's start by talking about what kind of issues you see as a problem and who makes the decisions about that problem."

Examples of Post-Racial Trauma Empowerment from a Veterans' Group*

- Choosing to leave a bed-and-breakfast early after experiencing poor treatment, rather than enduring it, as in the past.
- Engaging in a constructive dialogue with the leader of a Confederate flag group to share the perspective of what the flag represents to Black Americans.
- Creating a painting that includes a White military veteran, signifying significant healing from past racial trauma.
- Making the decision to relocate from a neighborhood after a decade of dissatisfaction, recognizing that the challenges were rooted in the community and culture, not personal character or qualifications.

** From Carlson et al. (2018)*

Social activism may be beneficial or take a toll on activists, based in part on their stigmatized identities. Some people benefit from activism, whereas others become burned out, underscoring the importance of moderation and self-care throughout activistic pursuits. In fact, some clients may seek treatment because their involvement in social activism led to racial trauma in the first place. In these cases, it's important to identify what specifically led to traumatization and what changes are needed to enable them to resume meaningful but non-traumatizing activism. It could involve reducing the time spent on activism, increasing social support, or finding a form of activism that is a better fit for their temperament.

Step 5: Assign Homework Exercises

Encourage the client to look for opportunities to promote anti-racist change in their environment (work, school, community). Have them write about systemic issues they have encountered and brainstorm about possible solutions. If they already have ideas, they can spend some time researching and writing about how they want to bring about that change and what that will require.

Between this session and the next one, the client should retake relevant symptom questionnaires to compare to baseline. This would include the RTS or the TSDS, as well as any other self-report measures where the scores were in the clinical range. They can complete the measures right after this session, do them at home and email them to you, or complete them online via your electronic medical record system.

Client reading in advance of the next session: Faber, S. C., & Williams, M. T. (2022, February 28). Children of color experience racism in German schools. *Psychology Today*. https://www.psychologytoday.com/us/blog/culturally-speaking/202202/children-color-experience-racism-in-german-schools

Therapist reading in advance of the next session: Bartlett, A., Faber, S., Williams, M., & Saxberg, K. (2022). Getting to the root of the problem: Supporting clients with lived-experiences of systemic discrimination. *Chronic Stress, 6*, 1–10. https://doi.org/10.1177/24705470221139205

Session 12: Goodbyes and Moving On

The goal of this final session is to synthesize the course of treatment and review mastery of techniques for purposes of relapse prevention.

Step 1: Review Homework

Start by discussing the client's efforts to identify opportunities for promoting anti-racist change in their environment, whether it's at work, at school, or in their community. Explore their observations of systemic issues and any solutions they brainstormed. Encourage them to share their experiences and reflections on this proactive step toward change. Discuss any challenges they encountered and any successes or new insights gained to help them further understand their role in confronting racism and systemic issues.

Next, inquire about the assigned reading, and ask them to share their thoughts and reactions. Encourage them to connect the article's content to their own experiences and the anti-racist efforts they're undertaking, if there is a connection. Finally, ask them how it was to retake the relevant symptom questionnaires, which you will have already compared to baseline measures before the session.

How to Know When Clients Are Ready to Move On

- They no longer fear experiences of racism.
- They have trusted people they can lean on for support.
- They are well equipped to deal with microaggressions.
- They don't internalize experiences of racism.
- They engage in regular self-care.
- They have a coping/recovery plan if racism knocks them down.

Image credit: © Kar-Tr; iStock

Step 2: Assessing Progress and Allowing for a Chance to Reflect

The final session should include a reflective exercise, giving the client an opportunity to look back on their journey of healing from racial trauma. Together, you and your client can revisit the initial goals set, the challenges faced, and the progress made. As you review their progress, make sure to explore the cognitive shifts, behavioral changes, and strategies that proved most effective for them against the stress and trauma of racism. Emphasize the transformative power of being able to understand the nature of racism, reclaim their trauma narrative, and implement empowering strategies as they move forward. By acknowledging the milestones reached, your client can more fully appreciate their resilience and growth. Some questions you can ask that may promote a discussion of their growth and change include:

- *How has your understanding of racism shifted after our meetings over the past few months?*
- *How have your behaviors changed?*
- *How do you respond to microaggressions now?*
- *How do you feel about those who oppress you now?*
- *Do you know that experiences of racism should not be internalized?*
- *How do you feel in your body and spirit?*

Step 3: Going Forward

While the therapy might be concluding, the journey of healing and personal growth continues. Racism is an ongoing problem that continues to evolve and shift with the times, so you should help equip the client with a plan for the future. This plan should include strategies the client can use to manage potential triggers and racial stressors, self-care practices they can do daily or weekly to maintain good mental health, and resources or support they can tap into when faced with challenging situations. The focus should be on fostering autonomy, allowing clients to take control of their healing beyond the therapy room.

Encourage the client to include techniques and exercises they practiced in sessions, like journaling or mindfulness exercises, as part of their ongoing self-care toolkit, based on what worked well for the client. Some questions you can ask to facilitate this discussion include:

- *How are you engaging in self-care and how will you continue to do so?*
- *How will you respond when an experience of racism happens?*
- *If you experience persisting distress, what is your recovery plan?*
- *How will you continue your healing journey?*
- *How can you help others in your community, workplace, or social networks to heal?*

Work with the client to synthesize their ideas into a concrete racial wellness plan they can take with them at the conclusion of therapy. This toolkit can serve as an easy-to-reference relapse prevention guide that will allow them to continue on their healing journey.

Racial Wellness Plan

The following exercise will help you identify strategies, self-care practices, and resources to maintain wellness in the face of racism after the end of therapy.

1. Recognize that racism is an ongoing issue that you will continue to encounter regularly. List places or situations you encounter where racism is most likely to occur.

2. Use the skills you've learned to recognize and push back against racism when it occurs. List the most helpful skills you've learned here.

3. Reach out to understanding friends for support when you experience racism. List at least four supportive friends or family members you can text or call to debrief from racism.

4. Continue regular self-care to stay strong so you can continue to be resilient in the face of racism and other life challenges. List three things you will do each week for self-care.

5. Stress is a normal part of life. You should not live in a constant state of stress but recognize that it will come and go. List any major stressors you anticipate over the next six months.

6. Accept that when you are under stress, it will make you more sensitive to racism and decrease your ability to tolerate it. Recognize that you are human and commit to exercising self-compassion. List some affirmations you can tell yourself when you need some self-compassion.

7. When you're under heavy stress, you need to spend time away from racial stressors to recharge. Turn off the news and social media—it will still be there when you are ready to re-engage! List some ways you can find sanctuary from racism when needed.

8. Traumatic racial stressors may emerge without warning. If you are experiencing symptoms of racial trauma that are not getting better, check back in with your therapist for some booster sessions. Write down what signs and symptoms indicate that you need to check in with a therapist.

Sankofa: Remembering to Go Forward

Sankofa is a principle derived from the people of Ghana that says one should remember the past to make positive progress in the future. Sankofa involves periodic rebirth and renewal. In the context of the therapeutic setting, the goal is to help a client return intellectually, emotionally, behaviorally, and spiritually to a place of truth, harmony, and peace in their life, building on past experiences.

Image credit: © Dmytro Donets; iStock

Step 4: Termination

The culmination of the therapeutic relationship is a significant moment for both the therapist and client. It's a transition that should be marked with gratitude, validation, and an open invitation for future support if needed. Reinforce the client's strengths and resilience, acknowledging their courage and determination throughout the process. Remind them that healing is nonlinear, and there might be days when they feel challenged, but they now possess the tools and knowledge to navigate those moments. While the structured therapy is ending, ensure the client knows that they're not alone and that you are available should they need you in the future. You might say something like:

> *"I really enjoyed getting to know you and learning from you. In fact, working with you has been profoundly enriching for me. I was inspired by your strength, resilience, and insights. I've learned so much from our time together, not just as a clinician, but as a fellow human being navigating this complex and diverse world. I value the trust you've placed in me, and I'm grateful for the time we've spent on this journey together. It has really been a privilege to be part of your healing process. Do not hesitate to reach out if you need anything in the future."*

You should also review any changes in the client's test scores and outline any remaining areas as targets for future work and growth. Finally, it can be useful to end with some sort of closing ritual. Consider any of the following options:

- Pour water on a plant as libations.
- Share a poem or short passage that describes the spirit of the journey.
- Read a quote that offers inspiration for the future.
- Give the client a symbolic small gift they can take with them as a reminder of their growth.
- Provide a symbolic certificate of completion.
- Blow out a commemorative candle that the client can keep.
- Share a cup of special tea together.

Conclusion

Although racial stress and trauma are common presentations in therapy, we know that few therapists have the resources or training to treat these issues. By reading this book—and perhaps you have already begun using this protocol with your clients—you have taken a critical step toward filling the gap in your own practice. You have shown that you are an empathy-centered therapist who is committed to supporting and empowering your clients of color, and you have learned the essential components to treat racial stress and trauma from a CBT perspective. However, it is important to continue educating yourself and consulting with experienced senior clinicians for ongoing growth and challenging cases. Keep in mind that racism changes over time, as do the demographics of our communities, so cultural competency requires ongoing, lifelong learning.

I also urge you to keep up-to-date with ongoing research and treatment advances in our field, as well as to interrogate the racial biases that all too often underlie these studies. Psychedelic-assisted therapy, which is discussed in the following callout, is one such area to explore.

Psychedelics for Racial Trauma?

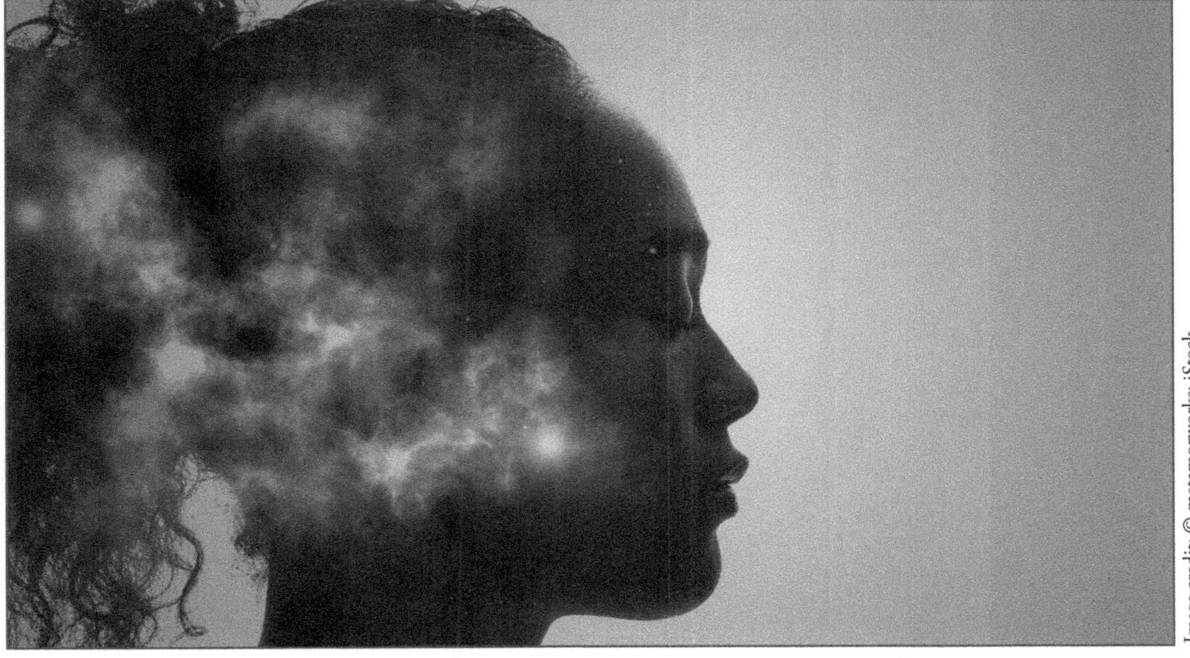

Image credit: © metamorworks; iStock

Ongoing research is being conducted on the use of psychedelics for treating different mental health conditions, including racial trauma. Psychedelic-assisted therapies can provide new insights and help resolve trauma. It is worth noting, however, that studies in psychedelic medicine frequently exclude people of color from their research cohorts, leaving a substantial gap in understanding how these therapies may affect these marginalized communities. This raises serious concerns about the ethics and efficacy of psychedelics in healing from racial trauma and their particular effects on people of color.

People of color face barriers to mental health care due to lack of cultural competency among providers and systemic racism in healthcare. As a result, some may turn to underground psychedelic use as self-medication to treat their own racial trauma outside traditional medical settings. Current research indicates that underground use can be helpful for racial trauma, but it also carries risks without proper precautions and support (Williams, Davis, et al., 2021). As new research into the potential benefits of psychedelics for racial trauma gets underway, it is important to remember these limitations and considerations if your clients are considering psychedelics as an adjunct to treatment. You may even see some clients who have heard the buzz and tried psychedelics on their own and are now looking for help making sense of the experiences. The techniques in this workbook can help with integration or be used as an adjunct to psychedelic-assisted therapy, with a therapist who is properly trained to deliver psychedelic-assisted therapy and is well-versed in anti-racist, culturally informed care (see Halstead et al., 2021).

Racism is a widespread problem that continues to evolve and shift with the times. Our ultimate goal must be to eliminate racism; however, the reality is that this will take time—and people need support *now* to manage racial stress and trauma. The protocol you have learned here is a practical way to support clients of color while we continue the fight to end racism. I wish you and your clients all the best as you carry on this journey toward healing, community, and justice.

Appendix

Culturally Informed Demographics Form (US Version)*

We want to be able to best understand the clients we serve, and the following questions help us get a better sense of who you are. We know that many of these categories may not fully capture the complexities of your individual experience. You will have more opportunities to discuss these questions with your therapist.

1. Name: ____________________
2. Street address: ____________________
3. City: ____________ State: ______ Postal code: ____________
4. Do you currently live in the United States? ❑ Yes ❑ No (*specify country*): ____________

   If not, how long have you been living outside of the US? ____________
5. Date of birth: ____________ What is your current age? ____________
6. What is your gender identity? (*check all that apply*)

   ❑ Male ❑ Female ❑ Trans ❑ Nonbinary, genderfluid, or genderqueer

   ❑ Not listed (*please specify, if you choose*): ____________
7. What is your sexual orientation? (*check all that apply*)

   ❑ No label (sexually open) ❑ Questioning ❑ Queer ❑ Bisexual

   ❑ Gay ❑ Lesbian ❑ Heterosexual ❑ Asexual

   ❑ Not listed (*please specify, if you choose*): ____________
8. What religion or spiritual practice (if any) were you raised with? ____________
9. What religion or spiritual practice (if any) do you identify with at present? ____________
10. What is the highest level of education you have completed?

    ❑ 8th grade or less ❑ Some college or 2-year degree

    ❑ Some high school ❑ College/university graduate (4-year degree)

    ❑ High school graduate or GED ❑ Graduate degree
11. Are you currently a: ❑ Part-time student ❑ Full-time student ❑ Not a student

* Adapted from Williams (2020a) and Suyemoto et al. (2016)

12. Are you currently involved in paid work?

- ❑ Not at all
- ❑ Working 1–20 hours per week
- ❑ Working 21–30 hours per week
- ❑ Working 31–40 hours per week
- ❑ Working over 40 hours per week

Please write in your occupation: ______________________________

13. Currently, your total annual household income (all earners) is:

- ❑ $0–$15,000
- ❑ $15,001–$25,000
- ❑ $25,001–$35,000
- ❑ $35,001–$50,000
- ❑ $50,001–$75,000
- ❑ $75,001–$100,000
- ❑ $100,001–$200,000
- ❑ $200,001–$300,000
- ❑ More than $300,000

How many people are supported by this income? ______________________________

14. Were you financially supported by someone else over the past year? ❑ Yes ❑ No

15. What languages do you currently speak? (*check all that apply*)

❑ English ❑ Spanish ❑ Other(s) (*please specify*): ______________________________

16. How fluent are you currently in English? (*circle one*)

Not at all fluent		*Moderately fluent*		*Completely fluent*
1	2	3	4	5

17. What language is currently spoken in your home most of the time?

❑ English ❑ Spanish ❑ Other (*please specify*): ______________________________

RACIAL AND ETHNIC BACKGROUND

We would like to get a complete picture of your racial and ethnic background to best serve you and ensure we are meeting our organizational goals of inclusivity. Because this information can be complex, we are going to ask you several questions about your race and ethnicity.

18. *Racial categories* are based on physical appearance (skin color and certain facial and bodily features) and presumed ancestry. These groupings have social meanings that affect how people see themselves and how they are seen and treated by others. Race is not the same as ethnicity or culture. The racial categories listed below are derived from the US Census Bureau. There may not be an option that represents your full identity, but for the purposes of this questionnaire, please indicate which **one group** below best describes your **racial identification**.

- ❑ Asian
- ❑ Black
- ❑ White
- ❑ Native American/Alaskan, American Indian, Native/Indigenous
- ❑ Pacific Islander, Native Hawaiian
- ❑ Not listed (*please specify*): ______________________________
- ❑ Middle Eastern, North African, Arab, West Asian (MENA; Non-White)
- ❑ Latinx/Hispanic (Non-White)

19. As noted, your racial identification may or may not match the categories above. In **your own words**, what is your racial identification? If you identify with more than one racial group, list all of them. ______________________________

20. How often do people perceive your race accurately? (*circle one*)

Hardly ever perceived correctly		*Sometimes perceived correctly*		*Always perceived correctly*
1	2	3	4	5

21. If you indicated that people sometimes or frequently do not perceive you correctly (selected 1, 2, or 3), please indicate the race that people most frequently perceive you to be: ________

22. People are often treated differently based on their skin color, which is called *colorism*. To best understand your experience, we would like to find out if you may be impacted by colorism. How would you rate your own **skin tone**?

    - ❑ Very light or pale
    - ❑ Light brown, tan, or olive
    - ❑ Medium or moderate brown
    - ❑ Dark brown
    - ❑ Very dark brown or black
    - ❑ Not listed (*please specify*): ______________

23. *Ethnicity* or *ethnic group* refers to a group of people sharing a common history, geographic background, and/or language, rather than their racial background. It might include things like values, patterns of interacting, food, dress, faith, holidays, or ways of seeing the world. There are hundreds of different ethnic culture backgrounds within the people in the United States—including Mexican American, Jamaican American, Filipino American, African American, European/White American, and more. You may have a Native American tribal affiliation that you identify with. We are interested in the ethnicity that reflects your heritage and life experience, which may be the heritage of your ancestors, if you continue to practice and identify with that ethnic group, but it may also be a more pan-American or global/international ethnicity.

    With which **ethnic group(s)** do you most identify? ______________________________

24. How much do you embrace the values in the ethnic group(s) you identified above?

Not at all		*Somewhat*		*Very much*
1	2	3	4	5

FAMILY AND GENERAL BACKGROUND

25. Where were you born?

    ❑ In the United States (one of the 50 states)

    ❑ In a United States territory (Puerto Rico, US Virgin Islands, Guam, American Samoa, Northern Mariana Islands, etc.) (*please specify which*): ____________________

    ❑ Outside the US or its territories (*please specify which country*): ____________________

26. If you were not born in the United States, how old were you when you came here? __________

27. What language(s) were primarily used in your home while you were growing up? (*check all that apply*)

    ❑ English ❑ Spanish ❑ Other(s) (*please specify*): ____________________

28. If a language other than English was used in your home growing up, how fluent are you in that language currently?

Not at all fluent		*Moderately fluent*		*Completely fluent*
1	2	3	4	5

29. In what sort of community were you primarily raised?

    ❑ Farm/rural

    ❑ Small town

    ❑ Medium-sized town/suburb

    ❑ Small city/large suburb

    ❑ Urban/large city

30. What is your current relationship status? (*check one*)

    ❑ Single ❑ Married ❑ Cohabitating

    ❑ Divorced ❑ Widowed ❑ Common law

    ❑ Separated ❑ Not listed (*please specify*): ____________________

31. To better understand important experiences in your life, it will help if you would be willing to answer a few questions about earlier sexual experiences that can be challenging to discuss.

    At what age did you have your first sexual experience? ____________________

    What was the relationship of the person you had it with? ____________________

    How old was that person? ____________________

    Do you feel that experience was due to force or coercion?

    ❑ Force ❑ Coercion ❑ Both ❑ Neither

Culturally Informed Demographics Form (Canadian Version)*

We want to be able to best understand the clients we serve, and the following questions help us get a better sense of who you are. We know that many of these categories may not fully capture the complexities of your individual experience. You will have more opportunities to discuss these questions with your therapist.

1. Name: ______
2. Street address: ______
3. City: ______ Province: ______ Postal code: ______
4. Do you currently live in Canada? ❑ Yes ❑ No (*specify country*): ______
   If not, how long have you been living outside of Canada? ______
5. Date of birth: ______ What is your current age? ______
6. What is your gender identity? (*check all that apply*)
   ❑ Male ❑ Female ❑ Trans ❑ Nonbinary, genderfluid, or genderqueer
   ❑ Not listed (*please specify, if you choose*): ______
7. What is your sexual orientation? (*check all that apply*)
   ❑ No label (sexually open) ❑ Questioning ❑ Queer ❑ Bisexual
   ❑ Gay ❑ Lesbian ❑ Heterosexual ❑ Asexual
   ❑ Not listed (*please specify, if you choose*): ______
8. What religion or spiritual practice (if any) were you raised with? ______
9. What religion or spiritual practice (if any) do you identify with at present? ______
10. What is the highest level of education you have completed?
    ❑ 8th grade or less
    ❑ Some high school
    ❑ High school graduate or GED
    ❑ College or 2-year degree
    ❑ University graduate (3- or 4-year degree)
    ❑ Graduate degree
11. Are you currently a: ❑ Part-time student ❑ Full-time student ❑ Not a student

* Adapted from Williams (2020a) and Suyemoto et al. (2016)

12. Are you currently involved in paid work?

- ❑ Not at all
- ❑ Working 1–20 hours per week
- ❑ Working 21–30 hours per week
- ❑ Working 31–40 hours per week
- ❑ Working over 40 hours per week

Please write in your occupation: ______________________________

13. Currently, your total annual household income (all earners) is:

- ❑ $0–$15,000
- ❑ $15,001–$25,000
- ❑ $25,001–$35,000
- ❑ $35,001–$50,000
- ❑ $50,001–$75,000
- ❑ $75,001–$100,000
- ❑ $100,001–$200,000
- ❑ $200,001–$300,000
- ❑ More than $300,000

How many people are supported by this income? ______________________

14. Were you financially supported by someone else over the past year? ❑ Yes ❑ No

15. What languages do you currently speak? (*check all that apply*)

- ❑ English
- ❑ French
- ❑ Mandarin
- ❑ Cantonese
- ❑ Arabic
- ❑ Tagalog
- ❑ Spanish
- ❑ Urdu
- ❑ Punjabi
- ❑ Not listed (*please specify*): ______________________________

16. How fluent are you currently in English? (*circle one*)

Not at all fluent		*Moderately fluent*		*Completely fluent*
1	2	3	4	5

17. How fluent are you currently in French? (*circle one*)

Not at all fluent		*Moderately fluent*		*Completely fluent*
1	2	3	4	5

18. What language is currently spoken in your home most of the time?

❑ English ❑ French ❑ Other (*please specify*): ______________________

RACIAL AND ETHNIC BACKGROUND

We would like to get a complete picture of your racial and ethnic background to best serve you and ensure we are meeting our organizational goals of inclusivity. Because this information can be complex, we are going to ask you several questions about your race and ethnicity.

19. *Racial categories* are based on physical appearance (skin colour and certain facial and bodily features) and presumed ancestry. These groupings have social meanings that affect how people see themselves and how they are seen and treated by others. Race is not the same as ethnicity

or culture. The following racial categories are derived from Statistics Canada. There may not be an option that represents your full identity, but for the purposes of this questionnaire, please indicate which **one group** below best describes your **racial identification**.

❑ East Asian (Chinese, Japanese, Korean)
❑ South Asian
❑ Southeast Asian
❑ Black (full or partial Black African origins)
❑ Indigenous (First Nations, Inuit, Métis)
❑ Filipino
❑ Latin American
❑ West Asian or Arab (Middle Eastern, North African)
❑ White
❑ Not listed (*please specify*): ______________________________

20. As noted, your racial identification may or may not match the categories above. In **your own words**, what is your racial identification? If you identify with more than one racial group, list all of them. ______________________________

21. How often do people perceive your race accurately? (*circle one*)

Hardly ever perceived correctly		*Sometimes perceived correctly*		*Always perceived correctly*
1	2	3	4	5

22. If you indicated that people sometimes or frequently do not perceive you correctly (selected 1, 2, or 3), please indicate the race that people most frequently perceive you to be: ______________

23. People are often treated differently based on their skin colour, which is called *colourism*. To best understand your experience, we would like to find out if you may be impacted by colourism. How would you rate your own **skin tone**?

❑ Very light or pale
❑ Light brown, tan, or olive
❑ Medium or moderate brown
❑ Dark brown
❑ Very dark brown or black
❑ Not listed (*please specify*): ______________

24. *Ethnicity* or *ethnic group* refers to a group of people sharing a common history, geographic background, and/or language, rather than their racial background. It might include things like values, patterns of interacting, food, dress, faith, holidays, or ways of seeing the world. There are hundreds of different ethnic culture backgrounds within the people in Canada—including Arab Canadian, Jamaican, Plains Cree, White/European Canadian, Singaporean Chinese, and more. You may have an Indigenous band affiliation that you identify with. We are interested in the ethnicity that reflects your heritage and life experience, which may be the heritage of your ancestors, if you continue to practice and identify with that ethnic group, but it may also be a more global/international ethnicity.

    With which **ethnic group(s)** do you most identify? ______________________________

25. How much do you embrace the values in the ethnic group(s) you identified?

Not at all		*Somewhat*		*Very much*
1	2	3	4	5

FAMILY AND GENERAL BACKGROUND

26. Where were you born?

❑ In Canada ❑ Outside of Canada (*please specify which country*): ____________________

27. If you were not born in Canada, how old were you when you came here? ____________________

28. What language(s) were primarily used in your home as you were growing up? (*check all that apply*)

❑ English ❑ Cantonese ❑ Spanish

❑ French ❑ Arabic ❑ Urdu

❑ Mandarin ❑ Tagalog ❑ Punjabi

❑ Not listed (*please specify*): ____________________

29. If a language other than English or French was used in your home growing up, how fluent are you in that language currently?

Not at all fluent		*Moderately fluent*		*Completely fluent*
1	2	3	4	5

30. In what sort of community were you primarily raised?

❑ Farm/rural ❑ Small city/large suburb

❑ Small town ❑ Urban/large city

❑ Medium-sized town/suburb

31. What is your current relationship status? (*check one*)

❑ Single ❑ Married ❑ Cohabitating

❑ Divorced ❑ Widowed ❑ Common law

❑ Separated ❑ Not listed (*please specify*): ____________________

32. To better understand important experiences in your life, it will help if you would be willing to answer a few questions about earlier sexual experiences that can be challenging to discuss.

At what age did you have your first sexual experience? ____________________

What was the relationship of the person you had it with? ____________________

How old was that person? ____________________

Do you feel that experience was due to force or coercion?

❑ Force ❑ Coercion ❑ Both ❑ Neither

University of Ottawa Racial/Ethnic Stress & Trauma Scale (UnRESTS)*

Guide for Interviewer		Interview Questions *(Instructions for the interviewer are italicized.)*
	A	***Introduction to the Interview***
Note the difference between race (the group society puts a person in based on their appearance) and ethnicity (a person's culture based on their heritage). They may be different or the same. *There are several officially recognized racial categories, including Black, White, Asian, and Indigenous. Hispanic is an ethnic group, but many consider Hispanic/Latine a race, which is acceptable for this interview.*	A1	Sometimes people have very bad experiences that cause feelings of stress or even trauma. Some people have several difficult experiences over a lifetime that are manageable individually, but together they lead to feelings of stress or trauma. I want to talk to you about some of your experiences of stress or trauma as it relates to your race or ethnicity. *If the patient's racial or ethnic group is unclear*: How would you describe your race and ethnicity?
Ensure that discussion only includes incidents where at least one of the involved factors was race or color.	A2	People may be discriminated against or mistreated for many different reasons (gender, sexual orientation, age, disability, faith, etc.) but I am interested in experiences connected to your race—or your race as perceived by others. However, if you have experienced discrimination due to a combination of factors (e.g., gender plus race, such a being called "an angry Black woman" because you stood up for yourself), we can talk about that too.
	B	***Racial and Ethnic Identity Development***
If yes, ask the patient to elaborate.	B1	Are there other racial or ethnic groups that people assume you belong to based on your appearance?
Ask the patient to describe this.	B2	When was the first time you became aware of race or ethnicity?
Ask the patient to describe this.	B3	When was the first time you remember feeling different, excluded, or singled out because of your apparent race or ethnicity?

* Updated version of the University of Connecticut Racial/Ethnic Stress and Trauma Survey (Williams, Metzger, et al., 2018)

Assess for things like positive messages from parents, racial socialization, negative messages from others, media, stereotypes, etc.	B4	What sort of things, positive or negative, did you learn about your race and ethnicity growing up? (*This may not apply to immigrants.*)
Assess for feelings of ethnic/racial pride and/or stigma/shame. *Rate each question (1–6) based on the patient's response.* *For each affirmative answer, solicit an example.* *For each negative answer, ask "why not?"* *Ethnic/Racial Identity Score (B5) Total:* ____________________	B5	I want to understand a bit more about how you feel about being a(n) (*enter race and ethnicity here*) ____________________ person. I'm going to ask you a few questions about that. **1.** Would you say that you feel strong attachment to your ethnic (or racial) group? *Very much (2) – Somewhat (1) – No (0)* **2.** Would you say that you have a lot of pride in your ethnic group and its accomplishments? *Very much (2) – Somewhat (1) – No (0)* **3.** Would you say that you are active in groups that include mostly members of your own ethnic group? *Very much (2) – Somewhat (1) – No (0)* **4.** Would you say that you have a strong sense of belonging to your ethnic group? *Very much (2) – Somewhat (1) – No (0)* **5.** Would you say that you think a lot about how life is affected by your group membership? *Very much (2) – Somewhat (1) – No (0)* **6.** Would you say that you have often talked to others about issues related to your ethnic group? *Very much (2) – Somewhat (1) – No (0)*
	B6	How much of your free time do you spend with people from your own racial/ethnic group?
Assess for a wish to be White, non-stigmatized, and/or a privileged group member.	B7	Many people note that it can be difficult to be part of an ethnic or racial minority. Have you ever wished you were a member of the majority group (i.e., a White person)?
Assess for composition of workplace/school and racial climate.	B8	What is the ethnic/racial environment like in your place of work/school? How comfortable do you feel there as a(n) (*enter race here*) person?

	C	***Experiences of Direct Overt Racism***
Give examples, if needed. This may include harassment at work, threats, victimization by law enforcement, etc. *Elicit a description of the event.*	C1	Can you share with me a time you were impacted by racism? This could be something that someone else either said or did to you. I am especially interested in any experiences where you were concerned about your safety and the event was very upsetting. *If needed:* If you can't think of any instances like that, then any racist experience will be fine (e.g., being followed in stores, being called racial slurs).
Determine when the event occurred.	C2	How old were you when this happened?
Be careful not to communicate doubt that this was in fact a racist event.	C3	What led you to believe this event happened due to your race?
Assess for the degree and type of distress experienced (e.g., anger, depression, anxiety).	C4	How upset were you by this experience? *If distress was present:* Are you still upset by it?
Determine if the experience was a trauma.	C5	Did you fear for your life, health, or safety? *If yes:* In what way?
Assess for adaptive versus maladaptive coping strategies.	C6	How did you cope with this experience?
Assess for availability and use of support systems.	C7	How did other important people in your life respond when you told them about this?
Ask about other experiences of racism.	C8	Can you tell me about another experience of racism like that? *If necessary:* This can be any other situation where you were fearful or concerned about your safety, or if the event was very upsetting.
Determine when the event occurred.	C9	How old were you when this happened?
Be careful not to communicate doubt that this was in fact a racist event.	C10	What led you to believe this event happened due to your race?
Assess for the degree and type of distress experienced (e.g., anger, depression, anxiety).	C11	How upset were you by this experience? *If distress was present:* Are you still upset by it?
Determine if the experience was a trauma.	C12	Did you fear for your life, health, or safety? *If yes:* In what way?

Assess for adaptive versus maladaptive coping strategies.	C13	How did you cope with this experience?
Assess for availability and use of support systems.	C14	How did other important people in your life respond when you told them about this?
	D	***Experiences of Racism by Loved Ones***
Elicit a description of the event.	D1	Can you share with me a time you were impacted by racism as a result of something that happened to <u>someone close to you</u>?
Determine when the event occurred.	D2	How old were you when this happened?
Be careful not to communicate doubt that this was in fact a racist event.	D3	What led you to believe this event happened due to race?
Assess for the degree and type of distress experienced (e.g., anger, depression, anxiety).	D4	How upset were you by this experience? *If distress was present:* Are you still upset by it?
Determine if the experience was a trauma.	D5	Did you fear for the life, health, or safety of that person?
Assess for adaptive versus maladaptive coping strategies.	D6	How did you cope with this experience?
Assess for availability and use of support systems.	D7	How did other important people in your life react to this?
Elicit a description of the event.	D8	Can you share with me another time you were impacted by racism as a result of something that happened to <u>someone close to you</u>?
Determine when the event occurred.	D9	How old were you when this happened?
Be careful not to communicate doubt that this was in fact a racist event.	D10	What led you to believe this event happened due to race?
Assess for the degree and type of distress experienced (e.g., anger, depression, anxiety).	D11	How upset were you by this experience? *If distress was present:* Are you still upset by it?
Determine if the experience was a trauma.	D12	Did you fear for the life, health, or safety of that person?
Assess for adaptive versus maladaptive coping strategies.	D13	How did you cope with this experience?
Assess for availability and use of support systems.	D14	How did other important people in your life react to this?

	E	**Experiences of Vicarious Racism**
Give examples as needed (e.g., shooting of an unarmed Black teen, racially motivated hate crimes, wars due to ethnic cleansing).	E1	Can you share with me a time you were impacted by racism as a result of something you learned about—for example, on the news or in your community—that involved someone you did not know personally?
Determine when the event occurred.	E2	How old were you when this happened?
Be careful not to communicate doubt that this was in fact a racist event.	E3	What led you to believe this event happened due to racism?
Assess for the degree and type of distress experienced (e.g., anger, depression, anxiety).	E4	How upset were you by this experience? *If distress was present:* Are you still upset by it?
Determine if the experience was personally traumatic.	E5	Did this event make you worry about your own well-being, health, or sense of safety?
Assess for adaptive versus maladaptive coping strategies.	E6	How did you cope with this experience?
Assess for availability and use of support systems.	E7	How did other important people in your life react to this?
	F	**Experiences of Covert Racism**
Microaggressions include brief exchanges, in the form of seemingly innocent and innocuous comments, subtle or dismissive gestures, and tones that send denigrating messages to people of color because they belong to a minority group.	F1	Often minorities are the target of subtle or covert racist experiences in the form of what we sometimes call "microaggressions." *Define if needed.* How often would you say that you experience these?
Elicit a description of the event.	F2	Can you give me a recent example?
Elicit a description of the event.	F3	Can you give another example?
Elicit a description of the event.	F4	Can you give another example?
	F5	How stressful is it for you when these sorts of things happen to you?
Assess for adaptive versus maladaptive coping strategies.	F6	How do you cope with these experiences?
	F7	Have you experienced any changes in your ability to manage microaggressions?
Note: Sections C–F may be duplicated to capture additional events.		

G. Racial Trauma Scale					
This scale allows you to determine the severity of racial trauma–based DSM-5 *trauma symptoms.* Think about all of the experiences we discussed concerning racism and discrimination as you answer the following questions. Answer each question in reference to the past month. *Note: For each positive response, ask for an example and then rate the item. Use all sources of information to formulate a rating, and do not read the anchors aloud.*					
Re-Experiencing *(Need 1 for a PTSD diagnosis)*	***Not at All*** *(almost never)*	***A Little*** *(once a week or less)*	***Somewhat*** *(2–3 times a week)*	***Very Much*** *(4–6 times a week)*	***Severe*** *(7+ times a week)*
G1. Have you had reoccurring, unwanted distressing memories about racism-related experiences?	*0*	*1*	*2*	*3*	*4*
G2. Have you been having bad dreams or nightmares related to racism, or about feeling powerless or excluded?	*0*	*1*	*2*	*3*	*4*
G3. Have you had the experience of feeling as if a past racism-related event was happening to you all over again (like a flashback)?	*0*	*1*	*2*	*3*	*4*
G4. Do you get very emotionally upset when reminded of racism-related experiences?	*0*	*1*	*2*	*3*	*4*
G5. Have you had negative physical reactions when reminded of racism-related experiences (e.g., stomachache, heart racing, shaking)?	*0*	*1*	*2*	*3*	*4*
Avoidance *(Need 1 for a PTSD diagnosis)*	***Not at All*** *(almost never)*	***A Little*** *(once a week or less)*	***Somewhat*** *(2–3 times a week)*	***Very Much*** *(4–6 times a week)*	***Severe*** *(7+ times a week)*
G6. Have you been trying hard not to think about upsetting racist experiences you've had?	*0*	*1*	*2*	*3*	*4*

G7a. Have you tried to avoid activities, places, things, or situations that remind you of the racism-related experiences you have had?	0	1	2	3	4
G7b. Have you tried to avoid certain types of people because you worry they will behave in a racist way (White people, law enforcement, bosses, etc.)?	0	1	2	3	4
Negative Changes in Cognition and Mood *(Need 2 for a PTSD diagnosis; count only one from G9 and/or G10)*	***Not at All*** *(almost never)*	***A Little*** *(once a week or less)*	***Somewhat*** *(2–3 times a week)*	***Very Much*** *(4–6 times a week)*	***Severe*** *(7+ times a week)*
G8. Are there any important parts of your experiences with racism that you cannot remember?	0	1	2	3	4
G9a. Have you been viewing yourself in a more negative way because of racism (e.g., "I should be a stronger person")?	0	1	2	3	4
G9b. Have you been viewing others in a more negative way due to racism (e.g., "I can't trust White people")?	0	1	2	3	4
G9c. Do you feel as if the world is a dangerous place because of your experiences with racism?	0	1	2	3	4
G10a. Have you blamed yourself for your experiences of racism, or for things that may have happened afterward due to racism?	0	1	2	3	4

G10b. Have you blamed others who were not involved for your experience, or for things that may have happened afterward?	*0*	*1*	*2*	*3*	*4*
G11. Have you had ongoing negative feelings such as fear, horror, anger, guilt, or shame because of your racism-related experiences?	*0*	*1*	*2*	*3*	*4*
G12. Have you lost interest in activities you used to enjoy?	*0*	*1*	*2*	*3*	*4*
G13. Have you been feeling detached, cut off, or alienated from other people?	*0*	*1*	*2*	*3*	*4*
G14. Have you had difficulty experiencing positive feelings? Or do you feel emotionally numb?	*0*	*1*	*2*	*3*	*4*
Physiological Arousal and Reactivity *(Need 2 for a PTSD diagnosis)*	***Not at All*** *(almost never)*	***A Little*** *(once a week or less)*	***Somewhat*** *(2–3 times a week)*	***Very Much*** *(4–6 times a week)*	***Severe*** *(7+ times a week)*
G15. Have you been more irritable or (physically or verbally) aggressive?	*0*	*1*	*2*	*3*	*4*
G16. Have you been taking more risks or doing things that might harm you or others (e.g., driving recklessly, taking drugs, having unprotected sex)?	*0*	*1*	*2*	*3*	*4*
G17. Have you been overly alert or on guard (e.g., checking to see who is around you, sitting in places where you can see everyone)?	*0*	*1*	*2*	*3*	*4*
G18. Have you been jumpy or more easily startled?	*0*	*1*	*2*	*3*	*4*

G19. Have you had a hard time staying focused or concentrating?	0	1	2	3	4
G20. Have you had a hard time falling asleep or staying asleep?	0	1	2	3	4
Dissociative Symptoms *Note:* These may be more likely when you get upset or stressed, especially when triggered by experiences of racism.	***Not at All*** (*almost never*)	***A Little*** (*once a week or less*)	***Somewhat*** (*2–3 times a week*)	***Very Much*** (*4–6 times a week*)	***Severe*** (*7+ times a week*)
G21. Do you ever have times that you feel detached from your body, disconnected from your sense of self, or like a robot? (*depersonalization*)	0	1	2	3	4
G22. Do you ever have times that everything seems rather unreal, dreamlike, distant, or distorted? (*derealization*)	0	1	2	3	4
Distress and Interference (*Need 1 for a PTSD diagnosis*)	***Not at All***	***A Little***	***Somewhat***	***Very Much***	***Severely***
G23. How much have these difficulties been bothering you? (*all symptoms discussed so far*)	0	1	2	3	4
G24. How much have these difficulties been getting in the way of your everyday life (e.g., relationships, work, school, parenting, or other important activities)?	0	1	2	3	4

Add total score (G1–G24 *all items*): ______________________________

G25. How long have you been feeling these things? ______________________________

For a *DSM-5* diagnosis of PTSD, in addition to a Criterion A event, the examinee must have:

- ☐ At least 1 symptom in the ***Re-Experiencing*** category
- ☐ At least 1 symptom in the ***Avoidance*** category
- ☐ At least 2 symptoms in the ***Negative Changes in Cognition and Mood*** category (count only one from G9 and only one from G10)
- ☐ At least 2 symptoms in the ***Physiological Arousal and Reactivity*** category
- ☐ At least 1 symptom from the ***Distress and Interference*** category
- ☐ A duration of disturbance (G25) greater than 1 month

Reference the *DSM-5* for exclusion criteria.

LIKELY DIAGNOSES: ______________________________

Notes about interview (optional): ______________________________

____

____

____

____

____

____

____

Trauma Symptoms of Discrimination Scale (TSDS)*

Instructions: When answering the following questions, keep in mind that discrimination is defined as: being unfairly treated due to an individual characteristic of yourself (e.g., race/ethnicity, gender, sexual orientation, religion).

PART 1: Frequency of Experiences
Experiencing discrimination can be very stressful, and sometimes people can feel specific types of stress due to discrimination that impacts their daily lives. This can be caused by one very stressful experience of discrimination, or several smaller experiences of discrimination over the course of one's life. Based on the experiences in your life, answer the following questions. Please keep in mind that ratings should reflect whether the type of stress was caused by discrimination.

Question	Never	Rarely	Sometimes	Often
1. Due to past experiences of discrimination, I often worry too much about different things.	1	2	3	4
2. Due to past experiences of discrimination, I often try hard not to think about it or go out of my way to avoid situations that remind me of it.	1	2	3	4
3. Due to past experiences of discrimination, I often fear embarrassment.	1	2	3	4
4. Due to past experiences of discrimination, I often feel nervous, anxious, or on edge, especially around certain people.	1	2	3	4
5. Due to past experiences of discrimination, I often feel afraid as if something awful might happen.	1	2	3	4
6. Due to past experiences of discrimination, I often have nightmares about the past experience or think about it when I do not want to.	1	2	3	4
7. Due to past experiences of discrimination, I often have trouble relaxing.	1	2	3	4
8. Due to past experiences of discrimination, I often feel numb or detached from others, activities, or my surroundings.	1	2	3	4
9. Due to past experiences of discrimination, I often avoid certain activities in which I am the center of attention (e.g., parties, meetings, answering questions in class).	1	2	3	4

* From Williams, Printz, & DeLapp (2018)

10. Due to past experiences of discrimination, I often cannot stop or control my worrying.	1	2	3	4
11. Due to past experiences of discrimination, I often find that being embarrassed or looking stupid is one of my worst fears.	1	2	3	4
12. Due to past experiences of discrimination, I often become easily annoyed or irritable.	1	2	3	4
13. Due to past experiences of discrimination, I often feel constantly on guard, watchful, or easily startled, especially around certain people or places.	1	2	3	4
14. Due to past experiences of discrimination, I often feel so restless that it is hard to sit still.	1	2	3	4
15. Due to past experiences of discrimination, I feel the world is an unsafe place.	1	2	3	4
16. Due to past experiences of discrimination, in social situations I feel a rush of intense discomfort, and may feel my heart pounding, muscles tense up, or sweat.	1	2	3	4
17. Due to past experiences of discrimination, I feel isolated and set apart from others.	1	2	3	4
18. Due to past experiences of discrimination, I avoid certain situations or speaking to certain people.	1	2	3	4
19. If I think about past experiences of discrimination, I cannot control my emotions.	1	2	3	4
20. Due to past experiences of discrimination, I am nervous in social situations and am afraid people will notice that I am sweating, blushing, or trembling.	1	2	3	4
21. Due to past experiences of discrimination, fear of social situations causes me a lot of problems in my daily functioning.	1	2	3	4

PART 2: Types of Discrimination Experienced

Below, please indicate the types of discrimination you have experienced in your lifetime. Please note that you must enter a corresponding percentage to the type of discrimination experienced. For example, if you've experienced discrimination due to your racial/ethnic background and gender, attach a percentage indicating how much of each you have experienced (e.g., racial/ethnic group = 70 percent, gender = 30 percent).

________ Racial/ethnic group	________ percent
________ Gender	________ percent
________ Sexual orientation	________ percent
________ Social class	________ percent
________ Religion	________ percent
________ Age	________ percent
________ Disability	________ percent
________ Other (list): ____________________	________ percent

Racial Trauma Scale (Clinical Version)*

Instructions: Think about all the times when you have heard about, seen, or experienced racial discrimination. As a result of this, how bothered have you been by the following:

	Not at All	*Slightly*	*Very Much*	*Extremely*
1. Thinking the world is unsafe	[1]	[2]	[3]	[4]
2. Feeling disconnected from myself.	[1]	[2]	[3]	[4]
3. Using alcohol to help me cope.	[1]	[2]	[3]	[4]
4. Feeling unsafe in public.	[1]	[2]	[3]	[4]
5. Having difficulties connecting with other people.	[1]	[2]	[3]	[4]
6. Using drugs to deal with my feelings.	[1]	[2]	[3]	[4]
7. Worrying about my loved one's safety.	[1]	[2]	[3]	[4]
8. Feeling nervous in social situations.	[1]	[2]	[3]	[4]
9. Using prescription medication to help with feelings.	[1]	[2]	[3]	[4]
10. Feeling society is unfair to people like me.	[1]	[2]	[3]	[4]
11. Fear that I will embarrass myself or others.	[1]	[2]	[3]	[4]
12. Causing myself physical pain (like cutting, burning, or hitting myself).	[1]	[2]	[3]	[4]
13. Thinking that others are purposefully working against me.	[1]	[2]	[3]	[4]
14. Feeling tired or as if I have less energy.	[1]	[2]	[3]	[4]
15. Sleeping too much.	[1]	[2]	[3]	[4]
16. Feeling watched by others.	[1]	[2]	[3]	[4]
17. Feeling worthless.	[1]	[2]	[3]	[4]
18. Weight changes without me trying.	[1]	[2]	[3]	[4]
19. Noticing people are less friendly to me.	[1]	[2]	[3]	[4]
20. Feeling like a failure.	[1]	[2]	[3]	[4]
21. Inability to stop moving.	[1]	[2]	[3]	[4]

* Reprinted with permission from "A Clinical Scale for the Assessment of Racial Trauma," by M. T. Williams, M. Osman, J. Gallo, D. P. Pereira, S. Gran-Ruaz, D. Strauss, L. Lester, J. R. George, J. Edelman, & L. Litman, 2022, *Practice Innovations, 7*(3), pp. 223–240. (https://doi.org/10.1037/pri0000178).

22. Feeling on edge around people who might be racists.	[1]	[2]	[3]	[4]
23. Thinking I cannot reach my goals.	[1]	[2]	[3]	[4]
24. Reacting angrily.	[1]	[2]	[3]	[4]
25. Avoiding certain situations or speaking to certain people.	[1]	[2]	[3]	[4]
26. Feeling like I am not as good as others.	[1]	[2]	[3]	[4]
27. Thinking about ways to make other people suffer.	[1]	[2]	[3]	[4]
28. Watching my surroundings for danger.	[1]	[2]	[3]	[4]
29. Feeling like I cannot succeed.	[1]	[2]	[3]	[4]
30. Having nightmares about discrimination.	[1]	[2]	[3]	[4]

Add all items (1–30) for a total score on the RTS. Total scores range from 30–120.

The three subscales are as follows:

(1) Lack of Safety: 1, 4, 7, 10, 13, 16, 19, 22, 25, 28

(2) Negative Cognitions: 2, 5, 8, 11, 14, 17, 20, 23, 26, 29

(3) Difficulty Coping: 3, 6, 9, 12, 15, 18, 21, 24, 27, 30

There is no time frame specified in the questionnaire, but clinicians can add their own time frame based on the needs of the assessment—for example: "As a result of this, how bothered have you been by the following *over the last two weeks*?"

References

For your convenience, purchasers can download and print the worksheets from **pesipubs.com/healingracialtraumaprotocol**

Abdulrehman, R. (2024). *Developing anti-racist cultural competence.* Hogrefe Publishing.

American Psychiatric Association. (2013). *Diagnostic and statistical manual of mental disorders* (5th ed.). https://doi.org/10.1176/appi.books.9780890425596

Anders, S. L., Frazier, P. A., & Frankfurt, S. B. (2011). Variations in criterion A and PTSD rates in a community sample of women. *Journal of Anxiety Disorders, 25*(2), 176–184. https://doi.org/10.1016/j.janxdis.2010.08.018

Atkinson, D. R., Morten, G., & Sue, D. W. (1998). *Counseling American minorities: A cross-cultural perspective* (5th ed.). McGraw-Hill.

Bartlett, A., Faber, S., Williams, M., & Saxberg, K. (2022). Getting to the root of the problem: Supporting clients with lived-experiences of systemic discrimination. *Chronic Stress, 6*, 1–10. https://doi.org/10.1177/24705470221139205

Beck, A. T., Steer, R. A., & Brown, G. K. (1996). *Beck Depression Inventory-II.* PsycTESTS Dataset.

Benuto, L. T., Singer, J., Newlands, R. T., & Casas, J. B. (2019). Training culturally competent psychologists: Where are we and where do we need to go? *Training and Education in Professional Psychology, 13*(1), 56–63. https://doi.org/10.1037/tep0000214

Bergkamp, J., O'Leary, S. M., Krizizke, J., Lash, M., Trantel, N., Vaught, J., Fulmer, T., Waite, I., Martin, A. M., Scheiderer, C., & Olson, L. (2023). Pathways to the therapist paragon: A decolonial grounded theory. *Frontiers in Psychology, 14.* https://doi.org/10.3389/fpsyg.2023.1185762

Bryc, K., Durand, E. Y., Macpherson, J. M., Reich, D., & Mountain, J. L. (2015). The genetic ancestry of African Americans, Latinos, and European Americans across the United States. *American Journal of Human Genetics, 96*(1), 37–53. https://doi.org/10.1016/j.ajhg.2014.11.010

Carlson, M., Endlsey, M., Motley, D., Shawahin, L. N., & Williams, M. T. (2018). Addressing the impact of racism on veterans of color: A race-based stress and trauma intervention. *Psychology of Violence, 8*(6), 748–762. https://doi.org/10.1037/vio0000221

Carter, R. T., & Forsyth, J. M. (2009). A guide to the forensic assessment of race-based traumatic stress reactions. *Journal of the American Academy of Psychiatry Law, 37*, 28–40.

Carter, R., & Pieterse, A. (2020). The short form and the interview schedule of the Race-Based Traumatic Stress Symptom Scale. In *Measuring the effects of racism: Guidelines for the assessment and treatment of race-based traumatic stress injury* (pp. 140–166). Columbia University Press.

Carter, R. T., Roberson, K., & Johnson, V. E. (2020), Race-based stress in White adults: Exploring the role of White racial identity status attitudes and type of racial events. *Journal of Multicultural Counseling and Development, 48*(2), 95–107. https://doi.org/10.1002/jmcd.12168

Cerdeña, J. P., Plaisime, M. V., & Tsai, J. (2020). From race-based to race-conscious medicine: How anti-racist uprisings call us to act. *The Lancet, 396*(10257), 1125–1128. https://doi.org/10.1016/S0140-6736(20)32076-6

Ching, T. H. W. (2022). Culturally attuned behavior therapy for anxiety and depression in Asian Americans: Addressing racial microaggressions and deconstructing the model minority myth. *Cognitive and Behavioral Practice, 29*(4), 723–737. https://doi.org/10.1016/j.cbpra.2021.04.006

Comas-Díaz, L. (2016). Racial trauma recovery: A race-informed therapeutic approach to racial wounds. In A. N. Alvarez, C. T. H. Liang, & H. A. Neville (Eds.), *The cost of racism for people of color: Contextualizing experiences of discrimination* (pp. 249–272). American Psychological Association.

Cooper, C. (2017, August 18). To the therapist who called me a "strong Black woman." *The Mighty.* https://themighty.com/topic/depression/therapy-racial-bias-strong-black-woman

DeLapp, R. C. T., & Williams, M. T. (2016, July 19). Proactively coping with racism. *Psychology Today.* https://www.psychologytoday.com/us/blog/culturally-speaking/201607/proactively-coping-racism

Donovan, B. M., Semmens, R., Keck, P., Brimhall, E., Busch, K. C., Weindling, M., Duncan, A., Stuhlsatz, M., Bracey, Z. B., Bloom, M., Kowalski, S., & Salazar, B. (2019). Toward a more humane genetics education: Learning about the social and quantitative complexities of human genetic variation research could reduce racial bias in adolescent and adult populations. *Science Education, 103*(3), 529–560. https://doi.org/10.1002/sce.21506

Evans, G. (2018, March 2). The unwelcome revival of "race science." *The Guardian.* https://www.theguardian.com/news/2018/mar/02/the-unwelcome-revival-of-race-science

Faber, S. C., & Williams, M. T. (2022, February 28). Children of color experience racism in German schools. *Psychology Today.* https://www.psychologytoday.com/us/blog/culturally-speaking/202202/children-color-experience-racism-in-german-schools

Foa, E. B., Ehlers, A., Clark, D. M., Tolin, D. F., & Orsillo, S. M. (1999). The Posttraumatic Cognitions Inventory (PTCI): Development and validation. *Psychological Assessment, 11*(3), 303–314. https://doi.org/10.1037/1040-3590.11.3.303

Foa, E. B., Hembree, E. A., & Rothbaum, B. O. (2007). *Prolonged exposure therapy for PTSD: Emotional processing of traumatic experiences: Therapist guide.* Oxford University Press. https://doi.org/10.1093/med:psych/9780195308501.001.0001

Foa, E. B., McLean, C. P., Zang, Y., Zhong, J., Powers, M. B., Kauffman, B. Y., Rauch, S., Porter, K., & Knowles, K. (2016). Psychometric properties of the Posttraumatic Diagnostic Scale for *DSM-5* (PDS-5). *Psychological Assessment, 28*(10), 1166–1171. https://doi.org/10.1037/pas0000258

Foa, E. B., McLean, C. P., Zang, Y., Zhong, J., Rauch, S., Porter, K., Knowles, K., Powers, M. B., & Kauffman, B. Y. (2016). Psychometric properties of the Posttraumatic Stress Disorder Symptom Scale Interview for *DSM-5* (PSSI-5). *Psychological Assessment, 28*(10), 1159–1165. https://doi.org/10.1037/pas0000259

French, B. H., Lewis, J. A., Mosley, D. V., Adames, H. Y., Chavez-Dueñas, N. Y., Chen, G. A., & Neville, H. A. (2020). Toward a psychological framework of radical healing in communities of color. *The Counseling Psychologist, 48*(1), 14–46. https://doi.org/10.1177/0011000019843506

Guhlincozzi, A., & Wallace, D. (2022). The Latine community and COVID-19: Nuances, experiences, and data. In M. Laituri, R. B. Richardson, & J. Kim (Eds.), *The geographies of COVID-19: Global perspectives on health geography* (pp. 97–108). Springer. https://doi.org/10.1007/978-3-031-11775-6_9

Haeny, A., Holmes, S., & Williams, M. T. (2021). The need for shared nomenclature on racism and related terminology in psychology. *Perspectives on Psychological Science, 16*(5), 886–892. https://doi.org/10.1177/17456916211000760

Halstead, M., Reed, S., Krause, R., & Williams, M. T. (2021). Ketamine-assisted psychotherapy for PTSD related to experiences of racial discrimination. *Clinical Case Studies, 20*(4), 310–330. https://doi.org/10.1177/1534650121990894

Hargons, C., Malone, N. J., Montique, C. S., Dogan, J., Stuck, J., Meiller, C., Sullivan, Q.-A., Sanchez, A., Bohmer, C., Curvey, R. M. G., Tyler, K. M., & Stevens-Watkins, D. (2022). Race-based stress reactions and recovery: Pilot testing a racial trauma meditation. *Journal of Black Psychology, 48*(5), 645–677. https://doi.org/10.1177/00957984211034281

Helms, J. E. (1990). Toward a model of the White racial identity development. In J. E. Helms (Ed.), *Black and White racial identity: Theory, research, and practice* (pp. 49–66). Greenwood Press.

Hemmings, C., & Evans, A. M. (2018). Identifying and treating race-based trauma in counseling. *Journal of Multicultural Counseling and Development, 46*(1), 20–39. https://doi.org/10.1002/jmcd.12090

Herman, J. L. (2015). *Trauma and recovery: The aftermath of violence—from domestic abuse to political terror.* Basic Books.

Hochschild, J. L., & Weaver, V. (2007). The skin color paradox and the American racial order. *Social Forces, 86* (2), 643–670. https://doi.org/10.1093/sf/86.2.643

Hogarth, R. A. (2019). The myth of innate racial differences between White and Black people's bodies: Lessons from the 1793 yellow fever epidemic in Philadelphia, Pennsylvania. *American Journal of Public Health, 109*(10), 1339–1341. https://doi.org/10.2105/AJPH.2019.305245

Holmes, S. C., Zalewa, D., Wetterneck, C. T., Haeny, A. M., & Williams, M. T. (2023). Development of the Oppression-Based Traumatic Stress Inventory: A novel and intersectional approach to measuring traumatic stress. *Frontiers in Psychology: Psychopathology, 14,* Article 1232561. https://doi.org/10.3389/fpsyg.2023.1232561

Huntley, R., Moore, R., & Pierce, C. (2017). *Journeys of race, color, & culture: From racial inequality to equity & inclusion.* New Dynamics Publications.

Iwata, M. (2020). Too dark. In N. Khanna (Ed.), *Whiter: Asian American women on skin color and colorism* (pp. 48–51). New York University Press.

Kolbert, E. (2018, March 12). There is no scientific basis for race—it's a made-up label. *National Geographic.* www.nationalgeographic.com/magazine/2018/04/race-genetics-science-africa

Kugelmass, H. (2016). "Sorry, I'm not accepting new patients": An audit study of access to mental health care. *Journal of Health and Social Behavior, 57*(2), 168–183. https://doi.org/10.1177/0022146516647098

Landrine, H., Klonoff, E. A., Corral, I., Fernandez, S., & Roesch, S. (2006). Conceptualizing and measuring ethnic discrimination in health research. *Journal of Behavioral Medicine, 29*(1), 79–94. https://doi.org/10.1007/s10865-005-9029-0

Leuchtgens, H., Albus, T., Uhlemann, C., Volger, E., Pelka, R. B., & Resch, K. L. (1999). Auswirkungen der Kneipp-Kur, einer standardisierten Komplextherapie, auf Schmerz, Lebensqualität und Medikamentenverbrauch: Kohortenstudie mit 1-Jahres-Follow-Up [Effects of Kneippism, a standardized complex therapy, on pain, quality of life and use of medicines: Cohort study with a one-year follow-up]. *Forschende Komplementärmedizin, 6*(4), 206–211. https://doi.org/10.1159/000021249

Liu, H. (2021). White allyship. In *Redeeming leadership: An anti-racist feminist intervention* (1st ed., pp. 141–156). Bristol University Press.

Maretzki, T. W. (1987). The Kur in West Germany as an interface between naturopathic and allopathic ideologies. *Social Science & Medicine, 24*(12), 1061–1068. https://doi.org/10.1016/0277-9536(87)90021-9

Mosley, D. V., Hargons, C. N., Meiller, C., Angyal, B., Wheeler, P., Davis, C., & Stevens-Watkins, D. (2021). Critical consciousness of anti-Black racism: A practical model to prevent and resist racial trauma. *Journal of Counseling Psychology, 68*(1), 1–16. https://doi.org/10.1037/cou0000430

Neff, K. D. (2003). The development and validation of a scale to measure self-compassion. *Self and Identity, 2*(3), 223–250. https://doi.org/10.1080/15298860309027

Neville, H. A., Worthington, R. L., & Spanierman, L. B. (2001). Race, power, and multicultural counseling psychology: Understanding white privilege and color-blind racial attitudes. In J. G. Ponterotto, J. M. Casas, L. A. Suzuki, & C. M. Alexander (Eds.), *Handbook of multicultural counseling* (2nd ed., pp. 257–288). Sage Publications.

Norton, H. L., Quillen, E. E., Bigham, A. W., Pearson, L. N., & Dunsworth, H. (2019). Human races are not like dog breeds: Refuting a racist analogy. *Evolution: Education and Outreach, 12*(1), Article 17. https://doi.org/10.1186/s12052-019-0109-y

Public Religion Research Institute. (2022, May 24). *American bubbles: Politics, race, and religion in Americans' core friendship networks.* https://www.prri.org/research/american-bubbles-politics-race-and-religion-in-americans-core-friendship-networks

Reed, S. (2019, January 10). *The damage of White feminism: An anecdote.* Chacruna Institute. https://chacruna.net/the-damage-of-white-feminism-an-anecdote

Roberts, R. E., Phinney, J. S., Masse, L. C., Chen, Y. R., Roberts, C. R., & Romero, A. (1999). The structure of ethnic identity of young adolescents from diverse ethnocultural groups. *The Journal of Early Adolescence, 19*(3), 301–322. https://doi.org/10.1177/0272431699019003001

Sheehan, D. V., Lecrubier, Y., Sheehan, K. H., Janavs, J., Weiller, E., Keskiner, A., Schinka, J., Knapp, E., Sheehan, M. F., & Dunbar, G. C. (1997). The validity of the Mini International Neuropsychiatric Interview (MINI) according to the SCID-P and its reliability. *European Psychiatry, 12*(5), 232–241. https://doi.org/10.1016/S0924-9338(97)83297-X

Statistics Canada. (2011). *Canada year book 2011.* https://www150.statcan.gc.ca/pub/11-402-x/2011000/pdf/ethnic-ethnique-eng.pdf

Statistics Canada. (2017). *Visible minority and population group reference guide, census of population, 2016.* https://www12.statcan.gc.ca/census-recensement/2016/ref/guides/006/98-500-x2016006-eng.cfm

Sue, D. W. (2010, November 17). Microaggressions: More than just race. *Psychology Today.* https://www.psychologytoday.com/us/blog/microaggressions-in-everyday-life/201011/microaggressions-more-just-race

Sue, D. W., Alsaidi, S., Awad, M. N., Glaeser, E., Calle, C. Z., & Mendez, N. (2019). Disarming racial microaggressions: Microintervention strategies for targets, White allies, and bystanders. *American Psychologist, 74*(1), 128–142. https://doi.org/10.1037/amp0000296

Sue, D. W., & Sue, D. (2013). *Counseling the culturally diverse: Theory and practice* (6th ed.). John Wiley & Sons.

Suyemoto, K. L., Erisman, S. M., Holowka, D. W., Fuchs, C., Barrett-Model, H., Ng, F., Liu, C., Chandler, D., Hazeltine, K., & Roemer, L. (2016). UMass Boston Comprehensive Demographic Questionnaire, Revised. Appendix in Wadsworth, L. P., Morgan, L. P., Hayes-Skelton, S. A., Roemer, L., & Suyemoto, K. L. Ways to boost your research rigor through increasing your cultural competence. *The Behavior Therapist, 39,* 83–89.

Tolin, D. F., Gilliam, C., Wootton, B. M., Bowe, W., Bragdon, L. B., Davis, E., Hannan, S. E., Steinman, S. A., Worden, B., & Hallion, L. S. (2018). Psychometric properties of a structured diagnostic interview for *DSM-5* anxiety, mood, and obsessive-compulsive and related disorders. *Assessment, 25*(1), 3–13. https://doi.org/10.1177/1073191116638410

Torres-Harding, S. R., Andrade, A. L., & Romero Diaz, C. E. (2012). The Racial Microaggressions Scale (RMAS): A new scale to measure experiences of racial microaggressions in people of color. *Cultural Diversity and Ethnic Minority Psychology, 18*(2), 153–164. https://doi.org/10.1037/a0027658

Tsai, M., Kohlenberg, R. J., Kanter, J. W., Kohlenberg, B., Follette, W. C., & Callaghan, G. M. (2009). *A guide to functional analytic psychotherapy: Awareness, courage, love, and behaviorism.* Springer Science + Business Media. https://doi.org/10.1007/978-0-387-09787-9

United States Census Bureau. (2015, March 3). *New Census Bureau report analyzes U.S. population projections* [Press release]. https://www.census.gov/newsroom/archives/2015-pr/cb15-tps16.html

United States Census Bureau. (2022). *About the topic of race.* https://www.census.gov/topics/population/race/about.html

Weathers, F. W., Blake, D. D., Schnurr, P. P., Kaloupek, D. G., Marx, B. P., & Keane, T. M. (2013). *The Life Events Checklist for* DSM-5 *(LEC-5) – Standard.* [Measurement instrument]. https://www.ptsd.va.gov/professional/assessment/te-measures/life_events_checklist.asp

Weathers, F. W., Bovin, M. J., Lee, D. J., Sloan, D. M., Schnurr, P. P., Kaloupek, D. G., Keane, T. M., & Marx, B. P. (2018). The Clinician-Administered PTSD Scale for *DSM-5* (CAPS-5): Development and initial psychometric evaluation in military veterans. *Psychological Assessment, 30*(3), 383–395. https://doi.org/10.1037/pas0000486

Wei, M., Alvarez, A. N., Ku, T.-Y., Russell, D. W., & Bonett, D. G. (2010). Development and validation of a Coping with Discrimination Scale: Factor structure, reliability, and validity. *Journal of Counseling Psychology, 57*(3), 328–344. https://doi.org/10.1037/a0019969

Williams, M. T. (2015, September 6). The link between racism and PTSD. *Psychology Today.* https://www.psychologytoday.com/intl/blog/culturally-speaking/201509/the-link-between-racism-and-ptsd

Williams, M. T. (2017a, April 29). Unfriendly skies: United Airlines and police violence. *Psychology Today.* https://www.psychologytoday.com/us/blog/culturally-speaking/201704/unfriendly-skies-united-airlines-and-police-violence

Williams, M. T. (2017b, September 4). Racism hides behind the small things people say and do. *Psychology Today.* https://www.psychologytoday.com/us/blog/culturally-speaking/201709/racism-hides-behind-the-small-things-people-say-and-do

Williams, M. T. (2018, December 31). Demanding diversity: Tolerance is not enough. *Psychology Today.* https://www.psychologytoday.com/us/blog/culturally-speaking/201812/demanding-diversity-tolerance-is-not-enough

Williams, M. T. (2019, January 19). Uncovering the trauma of racism: New tools for clinicians. *Psychology Today.* https://www.psychologytoday.com/us/blog/culturally-speaking/201901/uncovering-the-trauma-racism-new-tools-clinicians

Williams, M. T. (2020a). *Managing microaggressions: Addressing everyday racism in therapeutic spaces.* Oxford University Press.

Williams, M. T. (2020b). Microaggressions: Clarification, evidence, and impact. *Perspectives on Psychological Science, 15*(1), 3–26. https://doi.org/10.1177/1745691619827499

Williams, M. T. (2020c, June 13). What is Whiteness? *Psychology Today.* https://www.psychologytoday.com/ca/blog/culturally-speaking/202006/what-is-whiteness

Williams, M. T. (2022, January 9). Self-care for the chronic and demoralizing stress of racism. *Psychology Today.* https://www.psychologytoday.com/us/blog/culturally-speaking/202201/self-care-the-chronic-and-demoralizing-stress-racism

Williams, M. T., Cénat, J. M., Osman, M., Caldwell, K., Gallo, J., & Faber, S. (2024). Les microagressions raciales comme obstacles au traitement en soins cliniques [Racial microaggressions as barriers to treatment in clinical care]. *Canadian Psychology/Psychologie canadienne.* Advance online publication. https://doi.org/10.1037/cap0000383

Williams, M. T., Ching, T. H. W., Printz, D. M. B., & Wetterneck, C. T. (2018). Assessing PTSD in ethnic and racial minorities: Trauma and racial trauma. *Directions in Psychiatry, 38*(3), 179–196.

Williams, M. T., Davis, A. K., Xin, Y., Sepeda, N. D., Colón Grigas, P., Sinnott, S., & Haeny, A. M. (2021). People of color in North America report improvements in racial trauma and mental health symptoms following psychedelic experiences. *Drugs: Education, Prevention & Policy, 28*(3), 215–226. https://doi.org/10.1080/09687637.2020.1854688

Williams, M. T., Faber, S. C., & Duniya, C. (2022). Being an anti-racist clinician. *The Cognitive Behaviour Therapist, 15,* Article e19. https://doi.org/10.1017/S1754470X22000162

Williams, M. T., Faber, S. C., Nepton, A., & Ching, T. H. W. (2023). Racial justice allyship requires civil courage: Behavioral prescription for moral growth and change. *American Psychologist, 78*(1), 1–19. https://doi.org/10.1037/amp0000940

Williams, M. T., Feng, R. Y., Faber, S., & Abdulrehman, R. Y. (in press). Building a positive racial and ethnic identity: Implications for mental health and treatment engagement. In E. Goetter et al. (Eds.), *Optimizing treatment engagement processes in CBT for anxiety and related disorders*. Springer Nature.

Williams, M. T., Haeny, A. M., & Holmes, S. C. (2021). Posttraumatic stress disorder and racial trauma. *PTSD Research Quarterly, 32*(1), 1–9. https://www.ptsd.va.gov/publications/rq_docs/V32N1.pdf

Williams, M. T., Holmes, S., Zare, M. Haeny, A., & Faber, S. (2023). An evidence-based approach for treating stress and trauma due to racism. *Cognitive and Behavioral Practice, 30*(4), 565–588. https://doi.org/10.1016/j.cbpra.2022.07.001

Williams, M. T., Metzger, I. W., Leins, C., & DeLapp, C. (2018). Assessing racial trauma within a *DSM-5* framework: The UConn Racial/Ethnic Stress & Trauma Survey. *Practice Innovations, 3*(4), 242–260. https://doi.org/10.1037/pri0000076

Williams, M. T., Osman, M., Gallo, J., Pereira, D. P., Gran-Ruaz, S., Strauss, D., Lester, L., George, J. R., Edelman, J., & Litman, L. (2022). A clinical scale for the assessment of racial trauma. *Practice Innovations, 7*(3), 223–240. https://doi.org/10.1037/pri0000178

Williams, M. T., Osman, M., & Hyon, C. (2023). Understanding the psychological impact of oppression using the Trauma Symptoms of Discrimination Scale. *Chronic Stress, 7,* 1–12. https://doi.org/10.1177/24705470221149511

Williams, M. T., Printz, D. M. B., & DeLapp, R. C. T. (2018). Assessing racial trauma with the Trauma Symptoms of Discrimination Scale. *Psychology of Violence, 8*(6), 735–747. https://doi.org/10.1037/vio0000212

Williams, M. T., Sharif, N., Strauss, D., Gran-Ruaz, S., Bartlett, A., & Skinta, M. D. (2021). Unicorns, leprechauns, and White allies: Exploring the space between intent and action. *The Behavior Therapist, 44*(6), 272–281.

Williams, M. T., Skinta, M. D., & Martin-Willett, R. (2021). After Pierce and Sue: A revised racial microaggressions taxonomy. *Perspectives on Psychological Science, 16*(5), 991–1007. https://doi.org/10.1177/1745691621994247

Wyatt, J. P., & Ampadu, G. G. (2022). Reclaiming self-care: Self-care as a social justice tool for Black wellness. *Community Mental Health Journal, 58,* 213–221. https://doi.org/10.1007/s10597-021-00884-9

Yahr, E. (2014). Lupita Nyong'o named People's Most Beautiful Woman in the World. Here's how stars typically land the honor. *The Washington Post.* https://www.washingtonpost.com/news/arts-and-entertainment/wp/2014/04/23/lupita-nyongo-named-peoples-most-beautiful-woman-in-the-world-heres-how-stars-typically-land-the-honor

Yoon, H. (2020, March 3). How to respond to microaggressions. *The New York Times.* https://www.nytimes.com/2020/03/03/smarter-living/how-to-respond-to-microaggressions.html

Acknowledgments

It truly takes a village to develop a new treatment approach for mental health and wellness, especially when tackling a challenging issue like racial trauma. I would like to take this space to thank the many people who assisted in bringing this workbook to fruition. I first thank Tahlia Harrison for her work on early drafts of this manuscript, including formatting workbook exercises and developing engaging graphics. I would like to thank Manzar Zare for her research support, writing, editing, and assistance with example dialogues. I thank Angela Haeny and Samantha Holmes for their work on the protocol on which this workbook is based and for their help with early sample chapters for the publisher. I thank Sophia Gran-Ruaz for her work coordinating the research project piloting an early version of this workbook, which included the oversight of student therapists, participants, and clinical supervisors.

I thank Sonya Faber, Rehman Abdulrehman, and Chad Wetterneck for their encouragement, insights, inspiration, and guidance. I thank Naomi Faber for her riveting comic illustrations. I thank Somia Mohamed for being an amazing woman of color, professional role model, and someone who helped me navigate my own racial traumas. I thank my children for keeping me young and curious about the world.

And, finally, I wish to thank all my clients who trusted me with their stories and healing and who taught me about the experience of racism through their eyes.

About the Author

Monnica T. Williams, PhD, ABPP, grew up in San Jose, California, a multicultural community that fostered her love for cultural diversity. Her parents were both Civil Rights activists who grew up in the South under the weight of Jim Crow segregation. They attended university just as Black people across America were fighting for basic human rights and dignity. Her father's college roommate, John Lewis, was the esteemed late US Representative, and her mother protested at the US Capitol alongside Dr. Angela Davis.

Having grown up in Silicon Valley, Dr. Williams originally studied electrical engineering and computer science at MIT before deciding to dedicate her career to mental health. She obtained her doctorate in clinical psychology from the University of Virginia in Charlottesville. She is a board-certified licensed clinical psychologist and professor at the University of Ottawa, in the School of Psychology, where she is the Canada Research Chair in Mental Health Disparities. She has founded mental health clinics in Virginia, Kentucky, and Pennsylvania, and is currently the clinical director of the Behavioral Wellness Clinics in Connecticut and Ottawa, where she provides supervision and training to clinicians for empirically supported treatments.

Prior to her move to Canada in 2019, Dr. Williams was on the faculty of the University of Pennsylvania Medical School (2007–2011); the University of Louisville in Psychological and Brain Sciences (2011–2016), where she served as the director of the Center for Mental Health Disparities; and the University of Connecticut (2016–2019), where she had appointments in both Psychological Science and Psychiatry. Dr. Williams's research focuses on culture, racism, and psychopathology, and she has published over 200 scientific articles on these topics. Her current projects include the assessment of racial trauma, addressing barriers to treatment in obsessive-compulsive disorder, improving cultural competence in the delivery of mental health care services, and interventions to reduce racism. This includes her work as a principal investigator in a multisite study of MDMA-assisted psychotherapy for PTSD for people of color. She also gives diversity trainings nationally for clinical psychology programs, scientific conferences, and community organizations.

Through the Kentucky Psychological Association (KPA), Dr. Williams has served as the diversity delegate to Washington, DC, for the American Psychological Association (APA) State Leadership Conference for two consecutive years. Dr. Williams considers the Association of Behavioral and Cognitive Therapies (ABCT) one of her main professional homes. She served as the ABCT African American SIG leader for many years and as Chair of the Academic Training and Education Standards (ATES). She currently serves as an associate editor of the ABCT journal *Behavior Therapy*. She also serves on the editorial board of many other journals, including *Cognitive Behaviour Therapy*, *International Journal of*

Mental Health, *Journal of Obsessive-Compulsive and Related Disorders*, and *Cognitive Behavioural Therapist*. She is a member of the Scientific Advisory Board of the International OCD Foundation and co-founded their Diversity Council. She is on the accreditation panel for the Canadian Psychological Association (CPA). Her work has been featured in all major US and Canadian media outlets, including *NPR*, CBS, CTV, *Huffington Post*, and *The New York Times*.

PAGE 10, THE WEEKLY CHALLENGER, JUNE 25, 1970

Family Reunion

A Family reunion was held Monday, June 15, 1970 at the home of Mrs. and Mrs. Peter C. Williams, Sr. Sitting: Mr. and Mrs. Peter C. Williams Sr. and son Charles Erwin Williams. Standin from left of photo are: Peter C. Williams, Jr. A government employee, Wash-ington, D. C. Mrs. Jacqueline Hubbard and baby La'dee Hubbard. Mrs. Hubbard is a Senior Law Student of Boston University. Mr. and Mrs. James Williams and son Brenton James, Mr. James is a computer analyist - E. Lansing Michigan. Mrs. James (Sandra) is a student at Michigan State University. Mr. and Mrs. Bruce C. Williams and duaghters, Sonya and Monnica Williams. Mr. Bruce Willi-ams is a research Physicist with Fairchild Corporation in San Francisoc, California. The reunion was most enjoyable. (photo by W. L. Jones)

Photo: W. L. Jones, *The Weekly Challenger.*

Dr. Williams can be reached at **www.monnicawilliams.com** and the following:

- Twitter: **@drmonnica**
- LinkedIn: **https://www.linkedin.com/in/monnicawilliams**
- Facebook: **https://www.facebook.com/monnica.t.williams**
- Instagram: **instagram.com/drmonnica**
- Clinic website US: **https://www.bewellct.com**
- Clinic website Canada: **https://www.bewellpsych.ca**
- *Psychology Today* blog: **https://www.psychologytoday.com/us/blog/culturally-speaking**